Job Search Warrior

Jamie Soo

Job Search Warrior

©2018 Jamie Soo

All rights reserved.

Editing and design by James Harbeck

ISBN 9781983388453

Contents

INTRODUCTION	1
SECTION 1: PERSONAL GROWTH STRATEGY	5
Chapter 1 **Start Your Day Feeling Cool, Calm and Collected**	6
Chapter 2 **Reframe to Help You Move On**	11
Chapter 3 **Stay Positive**	15
Chapter 4 **Stretch Your Comfort Zone**	19
Chapter 5 **Cultivate Your Curiosity**	21
SECTION 2: JOB SEARCH STRATEGY	25
Chapter 6 **Seek Valuable Clues from Labour Market Trends and News**	26
Chapter 7 **Show Your Personal Brand to the World**	29
Chapter 8 **Disrupt Your Job Search**	33
Chapter 9 **Make the Most Out of LinkedIn**	37
Chapter 10 **Network Everywhere**	43
Chapter 11 **Put Your Best Foot Forward (Small Details Matter)**	52
Recap	58
SECTION 3: MY JOURNEY	61
Call Me Maybe	62
Poker Face	64
What I've Learned About Building Relationships	66
My Cosmic Journey	69

Gonna Fly Now	71
With a Little Help from My Friends	73
Tap Into Passion	75
Time Travel	78
Positive Vibes	80
Positivity… Let Me Count the Ways	82
Try	84
Taking Stock	87
Pearls of Wisdom	90
Launch	92
Walking Zombie	94
The Personal Touch	97
Elevator Pitch	100
Flourish	102
Wonder Story	104
Curious Story	106
Storybook Life	109
Different	111
Job Search Chronicles	113
Job Search Chronicles, Continued	115
Yoga Story	117
Ubiquitous Networker	120
Works of Beauty	122
Serendipitous Moment	124
Universal Truth	126

Playing Nice in the Sandbox	128
Know Thyself	130
Spirit of Christmas	132
Play It, Sam!	134
Smile	137
Put a Song in Your Heart	139
Confessions of a Newbie Worker	141
A Little Good News—Part 1	143
A Little Good News—Part 2	145
Window of Opportunity	148
Circles	150
Back to the Future	152

Job Search Warrior

Introduction

"Focus on what matters. Where attention goes, energy flows. Where energy flows, things grow."
—Marc and Angel Chernoff

This book is for job searchers who are looking for a job in the Canadian labour market. You could be an experienced Canadian labour force participant or new to the Canadian labour force—a newcomer or student.

Why "Job Search Warrior"? It draws on the warrior pose from yoga.

You can try the warrior pose at home. In a standing position, take a step forward. Position your back foot so that it's at a 90-degree angle from your front foot. Bend your front knee slightly so that it's over your foot. Stretch one arm in front of you and one arm behind you. Focus on seeing just beyond your outstretched fingertips.

A person in warrior pose is confident, focused and primed for action—they are exuding their best self. This book will help you, the job searcher, be your best self—and get the job that your best self deserves.

When searching for a job, it's easy to pay attention to negative thoughts like "I'm not good enough" or "I can't do this." When we pay attention to these thoughts, our behaviour follows—we become immobilized and give up trying.

What if we can turn these negative thoughts around and make them positive? When we have positive thoughts, we are more hopeful and confident about ourselves. We want to do things to help us move forward, and that could include doing something new or different in our job search.

This book has three sections.

In section 1, "Personal Growth Strategy," I talk about positive practices that I've been doing. This will encourage you to think about positive practices that you can do to help you to refuel, keep positive and rise to the challenges of a job search.

In section 2, "Job Search Strategy," I talk about the elements of a complete job search that you can incorporate into your own search.

In section 3, "My Journey," I chronicle my own thoughts and journey as a human resources professional and Job Search Warrior through my LinkedIn posts, which I refer to in the first two sections. These posts are in chronological order according to when they were written. Please note that I use "job searcher" and "job seeker" interchangeably in this book.

The job search is traditionally thought of as writing a résumé, applying and going for interviews. Job Search Warriors see things differently:

1) They continually work on themselves so that they are prepared to rise to the challenges of their job search.
2) They are open to disrupting their job search and doing something new or different if the traditional job search methods aren't producing results.

I've been an HR recruiter/generalist for more than 24 years. The greatest thing that I learned from this experience is understanding how a recruiter thinks. To a recruiter, small things matter—like calling the recruiter if you're going to be late for an interview or making sure that your cover letter is addressed to the correct company.

My purpose in life is to help people. Helping job searchers is especially meaningful to me. I have been a job searcher for 4 years when you patch together all the periods that I have been unemployed. I empathize with job searchers.

I'm going to tell you two big ideas in this book:

1) Take some time to focus on yourself and follow positive practices like journaling, walking, spending time with family and friends, etc. Once you refuel yourself, you increase the chance of seeing possibilities around you—maybe you'll do something new in your job search or identify a different career path to explore.
2) Do all the things that you already know and are comfortable with in your job search, but make room to do something new or different. I advocate a blended approach to the job search, which combines traditional and disruptive elements.

I invite you to link-in with me on LinkedIn and let me know how your job search is going.

Job Search Warrior

Section 1: Personal Growth Strategy

Chapter 1
Start Your Day Feeling Cool, Calm and Collected

- Focus on feeling cool, calm and collected. This helps you to identify new possibilities and opportunities around you.
- What time do you get up in the morning? Is this early enough? Do you have time in your morning routine to get everything done that you need to without feeling harried? Are there any positive practices that you follow in the morning? How do you get your body moving? How do you focus your mind?
- I've built up a morning routine of positive practices that take 10 to 12 minutes. As a job searcher, I attended an HR networking event that started at 9:30 a.m. I would get up early enough to do my morning routine, check my e-mails and leave in plenty of time to make it before 9:30.

On a typical morning I'm up by 6:30 a.m. and start my day with the thought, "It is going to be a great day."

I do stretches and yoga moves, including the warrior pose (see the Introduction). I say a Buddhist chant. Next I meditate. I say positive affirmations. I end with looking at my vision board.

My morning routine doesn't take long: 10 to 12 minutes.

I'm up early enough to go through the morning routine and to look at e-mails on my computer.

Here's some more detail on what I do. I present it to give you ideas and inspiration for your own routine. I encourage you to develop a routine that is meaningful and effective for you.

Yoga moves. When I was at university, I checked out the array of activities that I could participate in, like ballroom dancing, squash, fencing and yoga. Between ballroom dancing and yoga, I decided on ballroom dancing lessons. I have since hung up my dancing shoes, but I enjoy *Dancing with the Stars* on television. After university I still had my gym membership and I enrolled in squash lessons. I enjoyed squash and played a few games. Fencing fell off my radar. Recently I read an article about stretching your comfort zone and I was reminded about the time that I almost took a yoga class at university. Read **Yoga Story** (page 117) to find out what happened next.

Buddhist chant. I say a few rounds of this Buddhist chant in the morning: "Nam-myoho-renge-kyo." I act on faith about this chant's positive effects. I read about this chant in a book called *The Buddha In Your Mirror* by Woody Hochswender, Greg Martin and Ted Morino.

Buddhist philosophy has two important things to teach you as a Job Search Warrior, whatever your background:

1) **Self-empowerment.** The only thoughts or behaviour that you can control are your own. You can't change what other people think or do. Things happen that are beyond your control (e.g., your interview doesn't go well or you lose your job). You can empower yourself by reframing an experience, thinking what can you learn from that experience and possibly doing something different in the future. Out of struggle comes an opportunity to reflect and learn and do.
2) **Change.** In a job search a thought may cross your mind that you will never find a job. That isn't likely, because

life is always changing. Things aren't always "bad" nor are they always "good." Mixed in with the "bad" days will be the "good" days and vice versa. As a friend reminded me, "this too shall pass."

Meditation (box breathing). Box breathing is a helpful stress-release technique. It helps to slow down a racing mind. It can help you in a stressful situation like before an interview.

Box breathing is this: slowly breathe in through your nose (for a count of four)—hold (for a count of four)—slowly breathe out through your mouth (for a count of four)—hold (for a count of four)—repeat. Your eyes can be open or closed. For me, I close my eyes; I'm concentrating on my breath. I can feel my stomach expanding when I breathe in and contracting when I breathe out. I do box breathing as part of my morning routine and throughout the day as needed.

Positive affirmations. I say these positive affirmations to myself in my morning routine:

- "God, grant me the serenity to accept the things I cannot change, courage to change the things I can, and wisdom to know the difference." —Reinhold Niebuhr
- "Whatever the mind can conceive and believe, it can achieve." —Napoleon Hill
- "Don't ask yourself what the world needs. Ask yourself what makes you come alive and then go do that. Because what the world needs is people who have come alive." —Howard Thurman
- "Keep moving forward." —Robin Sharma
- "Focus on what matters. Where attention goes, energy flows. Where energy flows, things grow." —Marc and Angel Chernoff

I wrote a post called **Pearls of Wisdom** (page 90) that lists some of my other affirmations.

These phrases are positive and affirming to me. They're there if I need to lift up my spirits and keep up my positivity. I encourage you to keep a list of phrases that are positive and affirming to you. You can look at your affirmations or say them to yourself.

Vision board. A vision board is a collage of images that you make for yourself. Use images that are most meaningful to you. I look at my vision board as part of my morning routine. You can look at your vision board in the morning to help keep you inspired and focused on your goals or who you want to be.

Robin Sharma is the author of *The Leader Who Had No Title*. One day I was watching one of Mr. Sharma's videos about vision boards and was inspired to try it.

I started off with an 8½″ x 11″ piece of paper. I looked for specific images on the Internet. I cut and pasted these images onto the paper.

The purpose of my vision board is to remind myself of…

- Who I am—someone who wants to help other people
- Who I want to be—someone who appreciates things, someone who is curious about Buddhist philosophy, someone who is organized
- What I want to do—using my talents, walking/yoga/meditation for good health, reading for continuous learning, staying in touch with friends via coffee meet-ups

Follow-up
- Be on the lookout for quotations that are inspiring to you. Write them down and look at them in the morning to help keep you feeling positive. Share your favourite quotation as a meme on social media.
- Construct a vision board for yourself. Share with family and friends and use it as a way to keep yourself focused and accountable.
- Try the box breathing technique as a way to release stress.
- Arrange to do a work-out in the morning with a family member or friend to help keep you feeling positive and ready to rise to the challenges of your job search.

Chapter 2
Reframe to Help You Move On

- You will experience setbacks in your job search. "Reframing" a situation means shifting your perspective and reflecting on the positives that you can draw from the experience.
- What setbacks have you experienced as a job searcher (perhaps a job loss)? What were the circumstances? How have you reframed the situation? What did you learn from the situation? Has the setback encouraged you to take a different path?
- An example of a setback was my third job loss. After some reflection I realized that losing my job was not entirely bad because all I was focused on was work. I concluded that a work-life balance was very important and that work was a component in my life and not my entire life.

As you will read in **Window of Opportunity** (page 148), I lost my job in May 2018—my fourth job loss.

Thoughts of blame and recrimination crossed my mind, but I quickly realized that living in blame and recrimination would not get me anywhere.

I had no control over what happened with my job, but I do have control over my thoughts and actions—I decided to reframe the situation and think about what I learned from the situation.

I learned how to handle stress better.

I re-acquainted myself with box breathing, which I was first introduced to in a workshop. I discussed the box breathing technique in chapter 1.

Box breathing is helpful for job searchers. For example, you may want to try it right before an interview when stress is at its peak. If you are like me and find attending a large networking event to be stressful, you can try box breathing before you head out to the event.

I came across a University Health Network YouTube video series. This 4-part video series is called *Exercises for Stress Reduction and Deep Relaxation*. These videos feature an instructor who walks you through a series of exercises—watching these videos is like being in an actual class!

I learned how to organize my work better.

I came across an article by Tony Schwartz called "The 90-Minute Solution: How Building in Periods of Renewal Can Change Your Work and Your Life." Essentially, Mr. Schwartz suggests that you focus on an important task for 90 minutes, take a break, and repeat. He suggests that humans are not built to work 8 hours straight without taking breaks.

At work I focused my attention on a certain task and took a break when I felt I needed one. I got done what I needed to do and I felt great for my effort.

For job searchers, you may want to focus your attention on a task (like writing a cover letter) for a block of time, take a break, and repeat with another task or the same task.

I used the setback to set me on a different path.

After the latest job loss, I did some reflection and decided that I wanted to help job searchers and that I could reach many more job searchers if I were to write a book. Other factors that influenced my decision: I've been writing a LinkedIn blog on my job search experiences. My blog received positive interest. I realized that I could incorporate some of these posts into a book. One of my friends had her novel published, and her success encouraged me to write my book. And now here it is and you're reading it!

As mentioned at the outset, you will experience setbacks in your job search.

It may be helpful to let yourself feel disappointment after a setback, get it out of your system and try to move past the disappointment after a while. For me, being informed that I wasn't moving on to the next interview stage didn't make me feel good. Negative thoughts would cross my mind like "I'll never find a job" or "I'm not good at anything." I let myself think these thoughts, but I would remind myself that all is not lost— I'll get some rest and I'll feel better in the morning.

Job searchers need to be aware about self-care and not overdo the job search. Do the basic things and be mindful about getting enough sleep, drinking lots of water, watching your diet and doing some exercise. Take some time out for yourself and engage in activities that will recharge your batteries like going for a walk, playing a sport, enjoying nature, talking to friends and family, listening to music, engaging in yoga, watching a funny movie or treating yourself to ice cream or chocolate.

If a loved one were in distress, you would know how to comfort that person. Picture yourself as being that person in distress and be kind to yourself.

Take a look at my post **Positivity... Let Me Count the Ways** (page 82), which summarizes some of the ideas in this chapter and adds a few more. For example, what we may perceive as a snub may not have been the intention at all. We can reframe the situation and give the other person the benefit of the doubt.

This is an opportunity to open up a conversation and clarify what's going on.

> **Follow-up**
> - What are 3 to 5 activities that recharge your batteries? When was the last time that you did those activities?
> - In a scenario where you weren't the successful candidate for a job, how were you able to reframe the situation? What did you learn from the situation?

Chapter 3
Stay Positive

- Stay positive, believe in yourself and stay the course, for good things are bound to happen.
- As a job searcher, who has encouraged you to stay positive? What does it mean to you to stay positive? What inspires you to stay positive?
- One time an HR workshop facilitator commented that I had a nice smile. A smile implies being happy. I can tell you that I'm not always happy, but I am always positive. I see the bright side of things. Positivity is a particular way of viewing the world. I've developed a positive mindset that I describe in this chapter.

I get up each morning and think, "It is going to be a great day."

Every day I write at least one thing in my **appreciation journal.** This is something nice that someone has done for me or that I've done for someone else, something joyful that I've experienced or something that I accomplished. It could be anything at all. You have the freedom to define the parameters of your appreciation journal to your own specifications.

For each entry I start off with the phrase: "What I felt was a positive experience."

Here are just 12 of the daily entries from my appreciation journal from January 2018 to June 2018. It takes just 2 to 3 minutes every day to update my journal.

- January 29, 2018—I gave $5 to two subway performers for playing "Smile." Their performance lifted my spirits. I went into work humming this song. I wrote about this experience in a post called **Smile** (page 137).
- February 10, 2018—I referred a LinkedIn connection to an HR Consultant job. I like it when I have an opportunity to help.
- February 17, 2018—I enjoyed *Come From Away* at the Royal Alexandra Theatre. This musical made me proud to be a Canadian. I wrote about my favourite musicals in a post called **Put a Song in Your Heart** (page 139).
- February 22, 2018—A friend and I saw Susan Stewart perform stand-up comedy live in person. Times like these add up to a lifetime of memories.
- February 24, 2018—A friend in his 30s decided to take piano lessons for the first time—he inspired me to open the piano after 40 years. I reminisce about taking piano lessons as a child in a post called **Play It, Sam!** (page 134).
- March 3, 2018—I was happy to organize myself better by implementing the tickler system at work. I wrote about this feeling of accomplishment in **Confessions of a Newbie Worker** (page 141).
- March 5, 2018—I love this quote by Rollo May: "Finding the centre of strength within ourselves is in the long run the best contribution we can make to our fellow men." I discovered this quote while reading Robin Sharma's book *The Leader Who Had No Title*.
- March 17, 2018—I found a Mary Tyler Moore episode on YouTube that I hadn't seen before. It was like finding hidden treasure, because I thought I had already seen all the episodes!
- March 18, 2018—I was diagnosed with hyperthyroidism and happy that I didn't have anything more serious. I wrote

about this experience in a post called **A Little Good News** (page 143).
- May 23, 2018—I've always admired friends who can speak more than one language because they are a bridge between two cultures. I was inspired to write a post called **Circles** (page 150).
- May 27, 2018—I had a serendipitous moment when a former colleague spotted me on a subway station platform and came over to say "hello." It was 5 years since seeing this colleague.
- June 3, 2018—After my fourth job loss I was inspired to write a post called **Back to the Future** (page 152). This post is about looking at your past jobs to give you clues as to what job you may be interested in doing in the future.

Keeping an appreciation journal helps you to see the positive things in life. If you are aware of positive things, you may become more attuned to an opportunity that comes your way.

Similar to an appreciation journal, having a sense of awe and wonder for the things around you could help you become more attuned to an opportunity that comes your way.

I write about experiencing awe and wonder in these posts:

- **Universal Truth** (page 126)—The moral of this post is that you could put something out in the universe and have something returned to you manyfold. If you like Winnie-the-Pooh, you will like this post.
- **Serendipitous Moment** (page 124)—I happened to read the building directory in the building where I worked and found that a girl that I had known in high school had an office in the same building.
- **Works of Beauty** (page 122)—Being in the company of live butterflies at a butterfly conservatory reminded me of the

time that I attended a Van Gogh exhibition at the Art Gallery of Ontario. Both were awe-inspiring experiences.
- **Curious Story** (page 106)—I was encountering curiosity at every turn. I noticed an update on curiosity that a LinkedIn connection shared. At work I was organizing a workshop on curiosity that would bring curious people to the workshop. Curiosity encouraged me to meet up with a new LinkedIn connection who I hadn't met before.
- **Wonder Story** (page 104)—I was amazed that LinkedIn connections would accept my invitation to come and speak at a workshop even though I didn't know them very well and no compensation was involved.
- **Time Travel** (page 78)—I reconnected with a high school classmate 40 years later. The amazing part is that he remembered where we sat in class and that I tried to help him.

Helping people can bring about a positive mindset in both the giver and receiver.

In my post **Positive Vibes** (page 80), I talk about a time when my barber mentioned that he has arthritis. He wanted to ask the Arthritis Society for information, but he didn't have the phone number to call. I went home and decided that my barber could use a nudge to call. I went on the Arthritis Society web site and printed off some materials (including contact information). I returned to the barber shop and handed him the information. I was confident now that he would call.

Follow-up
- Are you ready to start a journal?
- What sort of things inspire awe and wonder in you?
- Are you involved in helping people in some way?

Chapter 4
Stretch Your Comfort Zone

- Stretching your comfort zone has several benefits: 1) It will help you to grow; 2) It will give you a positive feeling of accomplishment; 3) It will build your confidence to try something new in your job search.
- Have you stretched your comfort zone lately?
- In this chapter I provide a personal example of going out of my comfort zone.

In December 2016 I went out of my comfort zone when I signed up for an 8-week improv class at the Bad Dog Theatre Company.

Four factors led me to sign up for the improv class:

Awareness—I attended DisruptHR Toronto (a networking event) and heard an entrepreneur talk about improv classes that she was offering. If I hadn't heard this presentation, I would not have known about improv classes to be able to pursue it.

What's Your Why—I looked into myself and realized that putting myself "out there" or making myself vulnerable was exciting to me. When I was a child I had an early taste of being on stage—I was in two professional productions of *The King and I* and played one of the royal children. The idea of taking improv classes was intriguing because of my positive childhood experience.

Opportunity—The Bad Dog Theatre Company offered courses at a time that I was looking for—on the weekend.

External Push—A friend casually remarked that I wasn't very adventurous when it came to trying new food. The gauntlet was thrown down and I wanted to take him up on his challenge of trying something new.

Before each class I'd get butterflies in my stomach, because I didn't know what to expect. Once the class started, I relaxed. I'm glad I took the improv class and am stronger for it. I satisfied my curiosity as to what improv class was all about!

Follow-up
- Look for small opportunities to disrupt your routine—take a different route to the grocery store, sample a cuisine that you haven't tried before, brush your teeth using your non-dominant hand.
- What is on your bucket list of activities that would take you out of your comfort zone, but you are willing to try? What is one activity from that list that you will do in the next quarter?
- Do you need an external push to get you out of your comfort zone?

Chapter 5
Cultivate Your Curiosity

- Expect jobs to change with advances in AI technology. What once were in-demand skills may no longer be required. In this context, you will need to cultivate your curiosity and be open to learning new skills if you wish to compete in a changing labour market. Having a curious mind opens you up to seeing possibilities including identifying a new role for yourself.
- How do you cultivate your curiosity? Do you seek out learning opportunities such as reading articles or e-newsletters, watching YouTube videos, listening to podcasts, attending webinars, etc.?
- I start off with a personal example where I was curious about setting up a blog web site.

A State-of-Flow Learning Experience

I was writing posts on LinkedIn for a while.

I was curious about setting up a blog web site, so that more people would have access to my posts.

I decided to use the Blogger platform for my blog web site.

A long time ago I bought a book about blogging and never opened the book because setting up a blog seemed intimidating. This time was different—I was determined to set up a blog. I read whatever information I could glean from the book and from the Internet. I experimented with the platform. I was excited to see my blog take shape as I started to post.

I called my blog The Positive Pathfinder (thepositivepathfinder.blogspot.com).

I promoted the new web site in a couple of LinkedIn posts (e.g., **Launch**—see page 92), but unfortunately, the blog never took off.

You could say that the blog was not a success in that it didn't have the intended effect of attracting more people to my posts, but for me, it felt like a victory to go out of my comfort zone, try something new and see something to completion.

I experienced a state of flow where I was completely engaged and lost track of time while putting the web site together.

Setting up web sites isn't something that I would pursue as a line of work, but I know that writing a blog (which is something related) can put me in a state of flow.

Subscribing to E-newsletters

E-newsletters are free and provide an opportunity to cultivate your curiosity and learn something new. For the sender, e-newsletters provide an opportunity to share great content as well as to promote their book or course to their subscribers (which is called e-mail marketing).

I subscribe to several e-newsletters. Here are some of them:

- **Mayo Clinic** (newslettersignup.mayoclinic.com)—medical information provider
- **Eric Barker** (bakadesuyo.com)—Mr. Barker's web site notes that "this site brings you science-based answers and expert insight on how to be awesome at life."
- **Adam Grant** (adamgrant.net)—Professor Grant's web site notes that "(he brings) the most fascinating new ideas and evidence about work and psychology (to 85,000+ readers)."

- **Dr. Mike Bechtle** (mikebechtle.com)—Dr. Bechtle writes stories in a blog called Conversations about Living on Purpose.
- **Jacob Morgan** (thefutureorganization.com)—Mr. Morgan shares content (articles, videos, podcasts) on the future of work.
- **Great-West Life Centre for Mental Health in the Workplace** (workplacestrategiesformentalhealth.com)—I subscribe to "Take Your Break," which the web site describes as "weekly e-mails with break activity ideas for individuals and teams at work."

Unlocking Your Potential

I read a terrific article by Duleesha Kulasooriya and Maggie Wooll called "Unlocking human potential... Proactive practices for individual elasticity." The authors use an analogy of a tree to demonstrate how we learn.

We need roots, a foundation if you will, so that we can be receptive to learning. Activities like reflecting and meditation help to slow down our minds and make us receptive to learning.

Shoots on a tree are outer manifestations of growth. Activities that make us uncomfortable like going to an improv class or attending a meet-up help us to grow.

The authors suggest that roots and shoots are complementary activities like yin and yang—you can't have one without the other.

Follow-up
- Have you experienced flow or lost track of time as you engage in an activity that you enjoy? Can this activity be something you pursue as a line of work?
- Do you subscribe to any e-newsletters?
- Read Duleesha Kulasooriya and Maggie Wooll's article on unlocking human potential. What roots and shoots activities do you engage in?
- Set up a Google Alert on a subject that you are curious about.

Section 2: Job Search Strategy

Chapter 6
Seek Valuable Clues from Labour Market Trends and News

- Learning about labour market trends and news will help you to determine if there is a demand for what you would like to do.
- How do you currently get information on the labour market?
- In this chapter I show you three ways to learn about what's going on in the labour market.

Arrange for informational interviews and talk to people in your network who work in the occupation that you have an interest in. They can give you a realistic preview of what it's like to work in that occupation and the potential demand.

Keep abreast of the news for general employment trends and get a heads-up on companies that may be expanding into the area where you live.

Go to the Government of Canada web site (jobbank.gc.ca)—it has a wealth of information on the Canadian labour market.

Would you like a general overview of the Canadian Labour Market?

Navigate through **jobbank.gc.ca** → Explore Careers → Understand the job market: Trends & News. You will arrive at a web page for Canada where you can look at the following information:

- Job Vacancy and Wage Survey
- Unemployment Rates
- Employment Numbers
- Average Weekly Earnings

Would you like information on which companies are expanding or closing down in a particular province?

Navigate through **jobbank.gc.ca** → Explore Careers → Understand the job market: Trends & News. You will arrive at a web page for Canada. Click on a provincial button to find out labour market news for that province.

On the same page as the labour market news you can access other labour market information for that province, including:

- Labour Market Bulletin
- Economic/Environmental Scan
- Sectoral Profiles
- Occupational Outlook

Would you like to check on the outlook (or demand) for a particular occupation?

Navigate through **jobbank.gc.ca** → Explore Careers. You will arrive at an "Explore Careers" web page. Enter an occupation and location and receive information on median wage, occupational outlook, job postings and requirements.

Follow-up

Check out the Government of Canada web site for labour market trends and news:
- Economic/Environmental Scan—provides an overview of major socio-economic trends that can have an impact on the local and provincial economy and labour market. The report is released annually.
- Labour Market Bulletin—provides an analysis of the local labour market and an assessment of local employment-related events. The reporting period is monthly.
- Local and regional labour market events and announcements—the reporting period is weekly.
- Sectoral Profiles—provide an overview of recent labour market developments and outlooks for some key industries.

Do a Google search on "labour market trends and news Canada" and read a report.

Chapter 7
Show Your Personal Brand to the World

- "Brand" is a marketing term that applies to both companies and job searchers. A company's brand conveys a certain impression to customers. Your personal brand is your best "you" that you want to convey to the world.
- What do you associate with McDonald's? (Maybe speed, convenience, fast food, etc.?) What kind of brand or impression do you want people to have of you?
- Currently my brand is helping job searchers. I am conveying this brand through this book and through a LinkedIn Group I formed called "Job Searchers Canada," which is a networking group for job searchers and all other parties interested in the recruitment process—e.g., recruiters, résumé writers, job coaches.

Before you can convey your brand, first you have to "know thyself." Then you can convey your brand and exert your brand.

Know Thyself

Take some time to think about your values, interests, personality and skills.

Values—You can take a free quiz about your work values on the Government of Canada web site (jobbank.gc.ca/quizhome). When you finish the quiz, you will be shown your work motivators, your preferred work setting, how you like to interact with others and your work style.

Interests—Check out the web site My Next Move (mynextmove.org) for a free quiz that will help you to identify your work interests and which careers you might want to consider.

Personality—You can check out the VIA Institute on Character web site (viacharacter.org) for a free online survey that will rank your character strengths. (I talk about my experience with the VIA survey in a post called **Know Thyself** on page 130.)

Skills—To identify your skills: 1) Think about the skills that you employed in your past jobs; 2) Think about the things that others most often come to you about.

Read about my own experience of this:

- **Taking Stock** (page 87) includes a summary of the above ideas as well as some new ones.
- In **Tap Into Passion** (page 75), I describe an article that I read by Warren Berger called "Find Your Passion With These 8 Thought-Provoking Questions." One of the questions that Mr. Berger poses in his article is "What is your sentence?" In other words, how would you describe what you love to do and to encapsulate this in a sentence? I took up Mr. Berger's challenge and describe in my post what my sentence is. You can discover your purpose or what you are passionate about when you articulate your sentence.

Convey Your Brand

Now that you are more aware of what "you" are all about, you can convey your brand to the world via your résumé, cover letter and business cards and on social media such as LinkedIn and YouTube.

- A résumé and cover letter are marketing brochures for yourself. Employers form a less-than-positive impression of you if there are spelling and grammatical errors in these documents. Don't forget to proofread before sending.
- Business cards are a marketing tool. Any time you are talking to people, you are networking. It's helpful to carry business cards with you at all times just in case you need to hand one out.
- On LinkedIn you can convey your brand to people via your photo, headline and summary.
- YouTube is a great way to learn and share knowledge. A friend of mine reviews car cams on YouTube and has set up a viable business for himself.

You convey a brand via the way you dress. When you are interviewing at a company, take note of the way that people dress at that company. For example, you may not want to dress too formally at a company where everyone dresses casually.

You convey a brand via your body language. At an interview in Canada, shake hands before and after the interview, smile, make eye contact, sit in an upright manner and avoid fidgeting or crossing your arms.

Exert Your Brand

You can do things to increase your chances of getting your brand noticed and being disruptive in the process:

- Write a LinkedIn blog.
- I completed a Plum.io Talent Profile, sent it to some connections and mentioned what roles I was looking for—this was a way of keeping in touch. You can complete your Talent profile (for free) at plum.io/job-seekers. I wrote two posts on this experience called **Job Search Chronicles** on pages 113 and 115.

- Rakesh Kana and Trang Pham followed all the job search protocols in finding a job, to no avail. They decided to try something new and disrupted their job searches. They wore sandwich boards, stood in front of Union Station in Toronto and handed out their résumés in a pen. They were successful in finding jobs. (I found their story inspirational and wrote about their experience in **Gonna Fly Now** on page 71.)
- A recruiter friend wanted to get himself in front of a hiring manager. He sent the hiring manager an in-mail on LinkedIn and explained why the hiring manager needed to hire him. My friend was hired for the job.
- A friend sent customized personal profiles of himself to employers explaining why they should hire him as their product manager. This strategy got him noticed.

Think of ways that you can differentiate yourself from other job candidates (a.k.a. brand differentiation) and increase your chances of getting the job. There comes a time to overcome personal inertia and just do it.

I cover the issue of brand differentiation in a post called **Different** (page 111).

Follow-up
- How well do you know yourself?
- How are you currently conveying your brand?
- What can you do differently to exert your brand?

Chapter 8
Disrupt Your Job Search

- Disrupting your job search is trying something new in your job search other than reading job ads, applying online and attending interviews.
- Have you done something to disrupt your job search?
- In this chapter I tell you how I disrupted my own job search.

At some point your job search may feel interminable—it seems to go on and on and you have nothing to show for your efforts. I felt like that in my job search.

In October 2014 I connected with a person on LinkedIn. Immediately after we connected, this new connection suggested that I write a blog.

I told my new connection that I would let his suggestion percolate for a while.

Fast-forward a year later to 2015 and I didn't think my job search was going anywhere.

I revisited his suggestion to write a blog, because I was intrigued with the idea of trying something new in my job search.

Instead of committing myself to writing a regular full-fledged blog (which seemed daunting), I could handle writing a single post and seeing what comes of that.

On December 12, 2015, I published my first post on LinkedIn and called it **Call Me Maybe** (page 62). It's a career article written from my perspective as a job searcher.

Call Me Maybe is my most popular post to date in terms of the number of likes, comments and shares.

In 2015 I sent my post to J.T. O'Donnell (CEO & Founder of WorkItDaily.com). J.T. O'Donnell is a career coach who helps job searchers with their job search. Ms. O'Donnell shared my post with her large network and this helped to increase viewership of this post.

I like writing posts because I get to use the creative side of me.

Call Me Maybe was an especially creative process to go through because I combined several things that I was thinking about into that one post. For example, before writing **Call Me Maybe** I attended an HR workshop where the facilitator likened the job search process to dating. I thought of that remark in brainstorming a title for the post, which by the way is a song by Carly Rae Jepsen. I like to use song titles or names of movies or TV shows as titles for my posts. They provide a catchy title, don't you think?

This first post spurred me on to write the next post, then another and then another. After writing several posts, I could finally say to myself that I write a LinkedIn blog. Sometimes you just have to start small and build from there.

As job searchers you learn about the traditional approaches of searching for a job: looking over job ads, doing a résumé and cover letter, preparing for interviews, etc.

You may find that the traditional approach needs to be supplemented, i.e., you may need to disrupt your job search and try something new.

For me, that "something new" meant writing **Call Me Maybe** and progressing to writing a blog on LinkedIn.

Shortly after releasing my first post, I was asked if writing on LinkedIn helped me to find a job.

It's not just about whether LinkedIn will help you find a job. It has other benefits. Here are some of the things I have gotten out of writing on LinkedIn:

- I get to do something that I enjoy doing (which is writing), being creative and expressing myself. Maybe something that I've written is inspiring or helping someone in some way. It feels freeing when I write.
- I get an online presence that contributes to my personal brand. Recently a friend of mine introduced me to her friend at an event by saying that I write a LinkedIn blog. I was happy that my friend introduced me in that way. Yes, I would like to be known as someone who can write.
- Something that I wrote on LinkedIn prompted someone I did not know to contact me for a volunteer opportunity at the Top Talent Summit conference. The volunteer opportunity required that I arrive at the event at 7:00 a.m.! But on the positive side, I got to meet some new people and reconnect with some people I already knew. As I am wont to do, I made a few new LinkedIn connections from that event.
- One of my LinkedIn connections (an HR/career management consultant at The People Shoppe) saw a post that I wrote (called **Try**, page 84) and wanted to put this post on her web site. I of course said "yes" and I became a guest writer on thepeopleshoppe.com. I was happy to have an article of mine included on someone's web site! **Try** is a post that I wrote for job searchers I was working with at the time.

- The activity of writing encourages me to reflect on things. I learn something about myself in the process. For example, **Walking Zombie** (page 94) encouraged me to reflect on my experience at Combined Insurance. I've changed from someone who didn't pay attention to socializing to someone who now pays a lot of attention to socializing.
- I take the occasion of sending a LinkedIn post that I've written to reconnect or strengthen a relationship on LinkedIn. My posts become a conduit for building relationships. Sometimes my connection will like the post. If that happens, I want to reciprocate my connection's kindness, and I will like, comment or share something that they send out to their LinkedIn network. Writing a post encourages engagement on LinkedIn.
- I can take a link to one of my posts and drop it into cover letters. I've done this to illustrate a strength of mine.

Follow-up
How can you disrupt your job search and do something that is different for you? Here are some suggestions:
- Volunteer at a non-profit, conference or trade association, or on a committee or board of directors.
- Explore how social media (e.g., Twitter, Facebook, LinkedIn) can help you.
- Build a web site that showcases your talents.
- Network at a meetup.com event.
- Participate in religious services, clubs, sports leagues, parent-teacher associations, etc.
- Ask for informational interviews.
- Arrange coffee meet-ups with friends.
- Ask for a referral from people you know.
- Attend a class, course or workshop.
- Visit an employer and drop off your résumé.
- Cold-call.

Chapter 9
Make the Most Out of LinkedIn

- LinkedIn is a professional networking site that offers a free basic membership. It's incumbent for job searchers to get themselves on LinkedIn, to network and to avail themselves of LinkedIn's services.
- Are you currently on LinkedIn?
- I've been a LinkedIn member for over 10 years. LinkedIn offers a basic membership service and premium membership service. I've tried both services and concluded that the basic membership service serves my purposes well. I use LinkedIn as a CRM (customer relationship management) system to keep in touch with connections. I also use LinkedIn's publishing platform to write articles.

LinkedIn's Benefits for Job Searchers

- **Your LinkedIn profile gives you an online presence or brand.** You want to differentiate yourself from other job searchers. Through your profile you convey a certain impression to employers—what you do best or would most like to be known for. Pay particular attention to your photo, headline and summary, as these things are noticed first.

- **LinkedIn helps to broaden your network.** One day someone sent me a LinkedIn invitation from another country. I did not know this person, but I accepted the invitation because we had a connection in common and the sender and I both have HR backgrounds. My new connection was curious and asked me HR-related questions. I was happy to answer these questions. One day my new connection said that he would be visiting the Toronto-GTA area. We met in person and had a great conversation. Since connecting in 2017, we have kept in touch via Skype and he is one of my closest friends.

Without LinkedIn I would not have had the opportunity to get to know this person. As with all networking, you sometimes have to take a chance (accept a LinkedIn invitation from someone you haven't met) and nurture the connection (follow up with a question or meet off-line if possible).

- **LinkedIn helps you with intel.** Let's say that you have a job interview or an informational interview lined up with a company representative. Is the company representative on LinkedIn? If yes, does their work or educational background suggest any questions that you may want to ask? Or do you notice any commonalities between your backgrounds that you may wish to bring up during the interview?

    Pay attention to visible mode versus private mode. Keep in mind what privacy settings you have on and what you are comfortable with. If you are in visible mode and you visit the company representative's profile, they will be notified that you visited their profile. On the flip side, you are informed who specifically has visited your profile. If you are in private mode and you visit the company representative's profile, the company representative won't know that you visited their profile, nor do you know who specifically has visited your profile.

- **You may be able to find job leads on LinkedIn.** Someone in your network may share a job lead at their company. If the job lead is helpful to you, that is great news. But if the job lead is not helpful to you, you can help other people by "liking" the update and informing your network of the job lead.

- **You can look up company pages.** This is particularly helpful if you are going for a job or informational interview and doing some research on a company.

- **Follow a company or individual.** You will receive updates on both.

Unsolicited LinkedIn Invitations

Here are some things I look for when I receive an unsolicited LinkedIn invitation from someone I've not met. The things that I discuss below may be areas that you want to look at as they pertain to your own LinkedIn profile.

- **Truthful content.** I was sent an invitation where the sender said that they attended a college in Toronto and received an advanced degree. I checked the college web site and they don't offer that particular degree. I didn't accept the invitation. Be truthful in what you present on your LinkedIn profile. Not being truthful is a deal-breaker.

- **Photo.** I look to see if there is a photo of the sender. I would rather see a photo than no photo.

- **LinkedIn headline.** You can indicate what roles you would like to be known for or what you are good at.

- **LinkedIn summary.** You can tell a story of what's your why (who you are) or what it is that you do. Telling a story is captivating for the reader.

- **Number of connections.** I look to see how many connections the sender has. If the sender has a low number of connections, I am less inclined to accept the invitation. I think it's helpful if you aim to have 500 or more connections in your network.

  Tips for increasing the number of connections in your network:
  1) Invite everyone you know friends, family and colleagues to your network.
  2) Carry business cards with you to networking events—exchange business cards with people you meet and connect with them after the event.
  3) Customize your LinkedIn invitations.
  4) Find people who have designated themselves as a LION (LinkedIn Open Networker)—they are open to networking with everyone.
  5) Join a LinkedIn Group—ask a question or comment inside the group and connect with fellow group members.
  6) Read a LinkedIn post—engage with the author by liking, commenting or sharing their post; send the author a LinkedIn invitation and indicate that you like their post.

- **Mutual connections.** I am curious to see if we have any mutual connections; that could become a topic of conversation for me to ask the sender or mutual connection.

- **LinkedIn note.** It's always helpful if the sender adds a customized note as to why they are sending the invitation or the context of the invitation. If you send me a LinkedIn invitation and say that you have read my book or LinkedIn posts, I am certain to accept the invitation! (On the flip side, when I send an invitation, I always indicate context in the invitation—I would indicate where we met, or if we haven't met I would indicate why I would like to connect.)

- **LinkedIn activity.** I check to see the sender's LinkedIn activity. If there is very little activity, that tells me that the sender does not engage on LinkedIn very much and I wonder what value I may receive from connecting with the sender. By "engaging" on LinkedIn, I mean if a sender likes, comments or shares updates or if the sender writes original posts. When connections engage on LinkedIn, I'm learning something from them that I had not known before.

- **Recommendations.** I check to see if the sender has recommendations. The profile would more likely be legitimate if they have been able to gather recommendations. Something about the sender's personality can be gleaned from recommendations received.

Nurturing a connection. Here are some things that I do to engage with people and keep in touch (a.k.a. nurturing a connection). I use LinkedIn messaging a lot.

- Share an article that a connection may find interesting.
- Wish them a happy birthday or congratulate them on a new job or promotion or work anniversary.
- Offer to introduce two connections to each other.
- Like, comment or share their updates.
- Send them the link to a post that I wrote.

- Let connections know that I'm in transition.
- Share a job lead.

My ideas on LinkedIn networking are summarized in a post called **What I've Learned About Building Relationships** (page 66).

When you have a history of engaging with a connection, it is *much* easier to go for an "ask" from that connection in the future.

Follow-up
- How do you plan to build up to 500 connections?
- Nurture a connection by trying out one of my ideas.
- Do you have business cards? Carry a few with you to be ready to hand out if you network with someone.

Chapter 10
Network Everywhere

- Networking can take place anywhere and everywhere. Networking is talking with people like family, friends, colleagues or strangers. When you network with a stranger, someone has to take the initiative to strike up a conversation.
- Are you the one who strikes up a conversation first?
- One time I was on the subway and I saw some people wearing Toronto Blue Jays jerseys. I thought to myself that they must be going to the Jays game. I asked the people if they were going to the game and I wished the Jays good luck.

Networking can be in-person, on the phone or via messaging (e.g., LinkedIn).

Networking can be for the purpose of finding a job.

Networking is like tending to a garden. What may start off as a casual conversation may become something more meaningful with repeated interactions over time. Patience is indeed a virtue in establishing deep-rooted connections.

Networking for Introverts

I prefer networking meetings where I'm meeting people one-to-one. I like to get to know people and find out what their interests are. I was a regular attendee at an HR networking event. There were typically 12 to 15 people at these meetings. I enjoyed these meetings because there was an opportunity to talk to people one-to-one. It helps that the ambience was quiet and conducive to holding a conversation.

I've attended large networking events. I had to go against the grain of my nature and be more of an extrovert. After the event, although I felt exhilarated (because of adrenaline pumping all night long), I was also exhausted.

I attended a tech networking event that attracted more than 400 participants. This event combined a networking opportunity plus scheduled speakers plus vendors. I wanted to attend the event to meet people in the tech industry, but on the other hand I dreaded going because I wouldn't know anyone there. My fear was that I would be standing alone in a room where people seemed to know each other and I'd be the only person who wasn't talking to anyone—I'd be seen as a wallflower.

Here's how I solved a fear of networking:

- **Don't assume what other people are thinking.** There could have been other people at the event who also don't like large crowds or are afraid of what others may be thinking of them. Once I got to the event, it wasn't too bad—I looked out for people who seemed to have attended alone and I would strike up a conversation with them.

- **Get some helpful advice.** I came across an excellent book by Mark Rhodes called *How to Talk to Absolutely Anyone*. I like Mr. Rhodes' style of writing, which is very personable—it was like receiving helpful advice from your own personal coach. Another suggestion is to check out Mr. Rhodes' YouTube videos that are branded under the name of Massively Improve.

- **Take a friend to a networking event.** I invited a friend to a couple of Tuni Talks (a networking event). It was comforting to know that I would have someone to talk to. At one particular Tuni Talk, people were busily engaged and talking to each other. I noticed one gentleman who was standing alone and looking at his smartphone. I suggested to my friend that we approach this other gentleman. I struck up a conversation and discovered that we had some things in common such as an interest in workplace culture. We were already a second-level connection on LinkedIn, meaning we had people in common in our networks. This gentleman turned out to be like a coach who offered supportive likes and comments on my LinkedIn posts. You just never know who you will meet at a networking event— a casual conversation at a networking event can lead to something surprising and beneficial. I wrote about this experience in my LinkedIn post **My Cosmic Journey** (page 69).

- **Introduce people to each other at a networking event.** One year I attended a holiday party that was sponsored by an HR association. It was held at Casa Loma. I had so much fun at this event, because I got to introduce people who I knew to each other! I felt I had a purpose in connecting people to each other. I like helping people. I think I missed my calling of being the host at parties and making other people feel comfortable!

- **It's not all about me.** If you're afraid you won't know what to talk about at a networking event, one thing you can do is to ask your conversation partner questions that get them to talk about themselves. Always important to be present in conversations: maintain eye contact and don't look over your conversation partner's shoulder hoping to find someone else to talk to! Be attentive to your conversation partner and don't fool with your smartphone. Listen to understand what your conversation partner is saying and ask follow-up questions. Try not to interrupt—let them finish their thought. Try not to formulate your own response while your conversation partner is talking, because then you're not fully listening. (See **The Personal Touch** (page 97) for a summary of these ideas.) Don't overdo the questions and have your conversation partner do all the talking. Be prepared to talk about yourself. Conversations are a two-way street.

Coffee meet-ups. One way of maintaining friendships is by arranging meet-ups with friends once in a while at a coffee shop or food court. It's a good way to catch up and provide support to each other. While in-person networking is nice, it's not always possible. Other ways to keep in touch are by Skype, e-mail and LinkedIn messaging. A couple of friends post comments on my LinkedIn posts and we have a public conversation!

Board of advisors. Your board of advisors is your support network. Anyone who you feel is supporting you in your job search (e.g., family, friends) is on your board of advisors.

You can have guest advisors on your board of advisors. These people agree to meet with you to provide specific occupational advice in an informational interview. In an informational interview, you may want to ask questions such as the following:

- What's it like to work in a certain occupation?
- What skills, experience and training are needed to enter that occupation?
- What are the benefits and pitfalls for working in that occupation?

- Does the person (who you are networking with) like their job?
- Why did that person choose that occupation?
- Who may be hiring for that occupation?
- Who else should you talk to?
- What is the future demand for that occupation?

Meetup.com. I've attended a few meetup.com events. You meet a few people and connect with them on LinkedIn. I attended a meet-up on curiosity. Good things happened after just attending two of their events.

When I was working at the Ontario Society of Senior Citizens Organizations (OSSCO), I was looking for a speaker for an OSSCO workshop. I approached one of the organizers of the curiosity meet-up and he agreed to speak at our workshop! Another time the curiosity meet-up organizers offered an event on blockchain technology. I wasn't interested in attending, but I told a friend. That friend attended and he made an important connection. You just never know what may come out of attending a meetup.com event!

Networking Can Take Place Anywhere

- I was in a line-up at a Ryerson University event waiting for the BBQ lunch when I started talking to a Ryerson alumnus who was in the same line. We talked about how financial literacy should be made available in schools. Who knew that this person would go on to become a published author? I connected with him on LinkedIn shortly after that chance meeting and we still keep in touch.

- I was waiting for an elevator at work to take me from the 4th floor to the lobby. An elevator came, the door opened and I stepped inside. Someone from an upper floor was already in the elevator. This person seemed to want to talk and so a conversation ensued. We connected afterward on LinkedIn. (I discuss this experience in a LinkedIn post called **Elevator Pitch** (page 100).)

- You can network with recruiters at a job fair. A friend who is living in another country applied for a job located in Toronto, and that company happened to be at the job fair I was attending. I followed up for my friend and talked to a company representative at the job fair. I like to advocate on other people's behalf. (See **Ubiquitous Networker** (page 120).)

- I was attending my first-ever yoga class at a yoga studio and I arrived before the door was even open. A fellow yoga student was already there. We struck up a conversation and connected on LinkedIn. (See **Yoga Story** (page 117).)

Advocacy networking. How do you feel about cold calls? Do you find them easy to do? I don't like cold-calling very much, but there was a particular instance where I didn't mind cold-calling at all. I was working at the Ontario Society of Senior Citizens Organizations (OSSCO). I organized meet-ups where participants had an opportunity to network with each other and to hear an interesting speaker. I was tasked with cold-calling non-profit agencies and asking if they would advertise our event by putting up a poster at their agency. Everyone I talked to was very gracious. If an agency agreed to put up our poster once, I continued to keep in touch by sending posters for other meet-ups that we had. Occasionally I'd talk to some of these agencies by phone. From a single phone call, a relationship can develop and grow—you just never know. (My post **Flourish** (page 102) describes my experience with cold-calling at OSSCO.)

I found it easy to make cold calls when I was calling on behalf of someone else (an organization in this case). I didn't want to let OSSCO down and so I could overcome any hesitation that I might have. On the other hand, I find it difficult to cold-call if I'm calling for me. If I have to make a cold call for me, maybe I can think about the time that I was cold-calling on behalf of someone else?

Virtual networking. I'm usually open to trying anything new once.

- Mingle—In 2014, I participated in an online speed networking event where everyone signed on to a web platform at a designated time and we chatted with each other via e-mail. You only had a certain amount of time with each person, so you had to be a fast typist! I made a few LinkedIn connections from that event.

- Whitney Johnson's Initiative—Whitney Johnson is a keynote speaker/author. I subscribe to her e-newsletter. She organized a networking initiative where she connected two readers with each other and they could network with each other on Skype. I was paired with someone from another country. We had a nice conversation! I was reminded that we can find purpose in life by the work we do. I connected with my networking partner on LinkedIn. (I wrote a LinkedIn post on this experience called **With a Little Help from My Friends** (page 73).)

Christmas. I am one of the very few people who still send out Christmas cards. This is my way of touching base with people. I also send out e-mails during the holiday season to wish people in my network a Merry Christmas and Happy Holiday. This is an opportunity to spread some joy and keep in touch. (Please see my post **Spirit of Christmas** (page 132).)

I have an aunt who sends an e-card to my family on all Canadian holidays—this is her way of keeping in touch too.

Vulnerability and trust. I've learned that you show vulnerability by being real and sharing feelings or fears or anything else that makes us human. It takes strength to show your vulnerabilities. I wrote two posts related to vulnerability: **A Little Good News** (page 143) (about the time that I got sick with hyperthyroidism) and **Poker Face** (page 64) (where in a work context it may make you happier to show up to work as your real self). You can instil trust with others if you show your vulnerability over repeated interactions.

Networking can be for the purpose of finding a job. I was a successful candidate for a position at the Ontario Society of Senior Citizens Organizations because of networking (a friend referred me to the hiring manager), so it's important to keep networking in your job search toolkit.

For other positions (Johnson Matthey, CCH, Combined Insurance, Marberg Staffing, YMCA), I applied to an advertisement and was the successful candidate. It's important to apply to online jobs too.

At the Canadian Hearing Society I worked at a temporary job and was the successful applicant for an internal posting. An option for job searchers is to get your foot in the door at a company and apply for an internal job later.

Networking at work. Once you find a job, don't forget to network with your colleagues and direct supervisor. When you are at your job, it's important to check your ego at the door and be open to learning (see **Playing Nice in the Sandbox** (page 128)).

Follow-up
- Strike up a conversation with a stranger.
- Where do you currently network with people? Where else can you network?
- Have you obtained any of your past jobs through networking? Are you connected on LinkedIn to those referrals?
- How do you keep in touch with people after you have met them at a networking event?

Chapter 11
Put Your Best Foot Forward (Small Details Matter)

- After 10 steps of preparation, we are finally at the recruitment process, from the time that you submit your résumé and cover letter to a company to the reference checking stage.
- What you may consider a "small detail" and nothing to worry about, like typos in your cover letter or exaggerated statements on your résumé, will be perceived as a big deal by a recruiter. Proofread your cover letter and be honest on your résumé. Put your best foot forward in all stages of the recruitment process—small details matter.
- Are there any other examples that you can think of where a seemingly small detail may matter to a recruiter? I start off with sharing an example of what I thought was a small detail.

An employer asked if I was on Skype so that they could arrange an interview with me. I said that I wasn't on Skype and hoped that this was a one-off request.

It turned out that Skype was more popular than I thought. A second employer asked if I was on Skype—they wanted me to submit a video clip of myself. Again I said "no" to Skype and to the video clip.

At this point, with two missed opportunities, I decided I'd better learn more about Skype.

I asked a couple of friends for help, but they weren't on Skype either. I turned to a web site (GCFLearnFree.org) and found a helpful tutorial on Skype. I went to my local office supplies store, bought a webcam and got myself on Skype.

A third employer asked if I was on Skype. This time I could say "yes" and I had an interview.

Job searchers can decide to accept a job offer (or not), but otherwise they have very little control in the recruitment process.

Employers decide who to interview and who to hire. The reason for rejecting a job searcher's application could hinge on a small detail—but we will never know what that detail is.

Job searchers have control in what they choose to focus on.

Here are some areas that job searchers can focus on in the recruitment process:

Résumés. Can you verify everything that is on your résumé? If not, don't put that item on your résumé. Don't misrepresent yourself.

In your educational section where you list degrees, diplomas or certificates obtained, be able to verify these achievements by producing a copy of your degree, diploma or certificate or the transcripts behind them.

In the employment section where you list current and past employment, be able to verify past employment by lining up references who can vouch for your past jobs and what you did in them. A reference can be a supervisor, customer or colleague. You may not always be able to find a reference for a past job, so keep copies of T4s to show employers that you worked there.

Cover letters. Err on the side of caution and include a cover letter with your résumé unless the employer specifically asks for a résumé only.

At the time you apply. Check on LinkedIn to see if you have any first-level connections at the company that you applied to. If so, ask if they will refer you.

Keep track on an Excel spreadsheet of all companies that you apply to. If one of the companies you applied to calls, you can remind yourself that you applied by checking your spreadsheet.

The headings on your spreadsheet can include the application date, where you learned of the opening (Indeed, LinkedIn, Monster, etc.), job title, and comments.

In the comments column, indicate the date of your interview, date of testing and any other pertinent information. Note the questions that you were asked in an interview and how you responded—in future when you are invited to interview at another company, you can look back at your records and remind yourself of interview questions that you were asked before. You can take those same interview questions and practise how you would answer them for your upcoming interview.

On your computer, create a new folder of the company that you applied to and keep a copy of the job ad, your résumé and cover letter. If the company calls you for an interview, you can remind yourself of the details of the job posting.

Telephone or Skype interview. Make sure that everyone in your household knows that you will be doing a telephone interview or Skype interview. Minimize distractions as much as you can.

Ask the interviewer who is calling if the interview can be scheduled at a specific time later, so that you may prepare for the interview.

Send a thank-you note particularly for a Skype interview.

Testing in your home office. Make sure that everyone in your household knows that you will be doing some testing. Minimize distractions as much as you can. Don't misrepresent your abilities by having someone else do the test for you.

Interview. Prepare for the interview by researching the company. Check out the company's web site and LinkedIn company page. Do a Google search. Read the company's most recent annual report.

Review the job ad. What questions could the interviewer ask you based on the job ad?

Check out The Muse's article "How to answer the 31 most common interview questions" and practise answering those.

Here are some common interview questions:

- What do you know about our company?
- Tell me about yourself.
- Why do you want to work at our company?
- What are your strengths and weaknesses?
- What is your greatest achievement?
- What are you looking for in your next position?
- Why are you the best candidate for the position?

Anticipate being asked behavioural questions that begin with "Tell me a time when…" Answer using SAR: S (describe the Situation) + A (Actions you took) + R (Result of your actions). An example of a behavioural question is "Tell me a time when you had a conflict (difference of opinion) and what you did about that."

Come up with a few questions to ask the interviewer.

Check out the interviewer's LinkedIn profile. Do you have anything in common? What is the interviewer's background that led him or her to the current position?

Know your résumé backwards and forwards. You should have it memorized by the time you get to your interview.

Create a checklist for yourself of what you will need to bring to the interview:

- Bring a copy of your résumé.
- Do you have a portfolio (or any past work) that you would like to show the interviewer?
- Bring a list of references.
- Be clear on how to get to the interview and who to ask for.
- Confirm who you will be meeting with.
- Decide the night before what you will be wearing at the interview.

On the day of the interview, call the interviewer before the interview if you anticipate being late for the interview. Be kind to everyone you meet at the company, because you never know who has input into the hiring decision.

After the interview, send a thank-you note to the interviewer. Follow up with the interviewer in a couple of days if you haven't received a status update by then.

References. Ask potential references first if you can put them on your reference list.

If a potential employer asks for your reference list, give a heads-up to your references that they will be contacted. Tell them who will be contacting them, what job you interviewed for, and what the role will entail. You can send your references the job ad that you applied to.

If you are new to the workforce and have no work experience, you can ask one of your professors for a reference. Or, if you are a volunteer, you can ask the volunteer organization where you volunteer for a reference.

Branding considerations. Make sure that your voice-mail greeting is professional in the event that a recruiter leaves a voice-mail with you. On the flip side, if you are leaving a voice-mail with a recruiter, make sure that it is professional as well.

Follow-up
- Is your résumé error-free—no spelling or grammatical issues?
- Have you checked that the company name, address and addressee are correct in your cover letters?
- Do you keep a record of companies and job postings that you apply to?
- Compile a checklist of reminders for your interview.
- Make sure that your voice-mail greeting is professional.
- Keep copies of T4 slips.

Recap

It's not what you say to everyone else that determines your life; it's what you whisper to yourself that has the greatest power.
—Marc Chernoff

Which of two thoughts is more likely to move you forward: "Yes, I can" or "No, I can't"? What you think to yourself matters.

Cultivate Positivity and See Possibilities Around You

Cultivate positivity with these positive practices:

- Have a morning routine and engage in activities that make you feel calm and centred.
- Reframe or shift your perspective so that you can draw the positives from a negative situation.
- Keep a daily appreciation journal where you record your moments of positivity.
- Take regular breaks from your job search and do something that energizes you.
- Do something that is out of your comfort zone and feel a glow of positivity from your accomplishment.
- Awaken your curiosity and explore a subject that interests you.

Once you refuel yourself, you increase the chance of seeing possibilities around you.

A Complete Job Search Toolkit Includes Both Traditional and Disruptive Elements

Look at the list of elements below and incorporate any element that is missing from your job search toolkit.

Traditional Elements

- Seek valuable clues from labour market trends and news.
- Show your personal brand to the world.
- Make the most out of LinkedIn.
- Network everywhere.
- Attend to small details—recruiters do.

Disruptive Element

- Do something new or different in your job search.

Characteristics of Job Search Warriors

- They are confident, focused and primed for action.
- They continually work on themselves so that they are prepared to rise to the challenges of their job search. Once they commit to a certain positive practice, they stick to it.

Final Thought

What will you do differently to become more like a Job Search Warrior?

Good luck as you embark on your journey of becoming a Job Search Warrior. Let me know how it goes.

Section 3: My Journey

Call Me Maybe

I confess: I am a Job Seeker.

A certain perception comes to mind when you tell someone that you're a "Job Seeker in Transition."

I'm not exactly sure what that perception is (because no one has really told me), but I'm here to tell you about the positive qualities of a Job Seeker.

We are resourceful. We feel like a number in an Applicant Tracking System, one of many candidates. And so, we do things to get an employer's attention like calling, sending an e-mail or even writing a post on LinkedIn!

We are empathetic. We know what it's like to be a job seeker, so if you hire us as a Recruiter, we will be kind to candidates and treat them the way that we would like to be treated. After all, the candidate with whom we are tweeting or talking to can be a potential star employee or happy customer with the company.

We are resilient. At some point in the process, our job search feels unproductive. I think back to one of my mentors who said that there will always be challenging times in our lives and that we always manage somehow to get through them. I suppose that all we need is positive thinking, some patience and to recharge our batteries once in awhile and do the things that will keep us happy and healthy (like talk with friends, read, go for a walk, meditate or have some dark chocolate)!

To my fellow Job Seekers, I would like to remind you to keep the faith and that YOU ARE AWESOME! I celebrate you for being you. There is no one else in this world who has your particular skills, interests and experiences. I love this quote: "Be who you are and say what you feel, because those who mind don't matter and those who matter don't mind." BE YOURSELF (and be true to who you are) throughout the job search process.

So, how about it, employers? Check out my LinkedIn profile and Call Me Maybe (with a nod to Carly Rae Jepsen)!

And, please don't forget to be kind to my fellow Job Seeker friends!

Poker Face

We show different sides of our persona (or personality) at work and at home.

When I reflect back at a previous company that I worked for, in HR, my persona was to be open and friendly. My immediate work group was good because we talked about our personal lives with each other. I was happy where I worked because I was being myself.

In everything there is a yin and yang. I was maybe too happy where I worked. By the time I got home from work, I was exhausted from working voluntary overtime. I brought work home with me to do on the weekends. I didn't see the importance of networking outside the company or making friendships outside of work.

Things change when you're a job seeker. You no longer have a place to go to every day, but you do have time to reflect. I see now the importance of networking (both inside and outside of a company) and the importance of making friendships.

A company that supports a positive workplace culture resonates with me. I've seen company web sites that say that they encourage employees to bring all of themselves to work. I think this is a great idea! We would be much happier (and perhaps more productive) if we could bring all of ourselves to work. "Bringing all of ourselves to work" has multiple meanings—it could mean sharing things with our colleagues like our personal interests, our family relationships, or things that are causing us anxiety or depression, etc.

When companies offer social events at their companies, these are not frivolous activities, because it is at these events that we can learn more about our colleagues and develop camaraderie. When we get to know someone, this opens up a greater possibility to collaborate in the future. We are more likely to want to share things with someone we know rather than with someone we don't know. On a personal level, when I talk to friends, I would like to know what's going on with them, because maybe I can offer an anecdote or advice or I could just be there to listen. On a later date, I'd follow up to ask how something that they talked about turned out. I like to form personal connections both at work and outside of work.

I read a terrific article by Ash Read called "What Does It Mean to Bring Your 'Whole Self' to Work?" Mr. Read talks about how many of us check our "real" selves at the door when we go to work or when we go home. I relate to his thoughts on vulnerability and reflection. Writing about what I think seems risky and it makes me feel vulnerable. But I think if you want to project your brand, you have to take the plunge and make yourself vulnerable. As a job seeker, I've had time to reflect and I reflect on things before I actually write a post.

I love the song "Poker Face" (with a nod to Lady Gaga), but in terms of our work and home lives, maybe we need to have less of a poker face and bring our best and real selves to work and at home.

What I've Learned About Building Relationships

One of my favourite workplace comedy movies is "The Devil Wears Prada."

There is a quote from this movie that I like.

For those who haven't seen "The Devil Wears Prada", this movie stars Meryl Streep (who plays Miranda Priestly) and Anne Hathaway (who plays Andrea "Andy" Sachs). Miranda is the editor of a fashion magazine who hires Andy as her personal assistant. Working at a fashion magazine is not Andy's idea of a dream job, but she commits to her job wholeheartedly and takes calls from her boss outside of working hours. Andy's commitment to her job starts to wear thin on her boyfriend Nate Cooper (who is played by Adrian Grenier).

In one scene Andy and Nate are having a conversation, and their conversation is interrupted with a phone call from Miranda. Andy decides to take the call, much to the chagrin of Nate.

Nate makes the following remark as Andy takes a call from Miranda:

"You know, in case you were wondering—the person whose calls you always take? That's the relationship you're in. I hope you two are very happy together."

I think Nate makes a very good observation.

You are in a relationship if you are wiling to take calls (or even e-mails) from someone. The opposite holds true as well, i.e., you're not in a relationship if you're not willing to take calls or respond to e-mails from someone.

As a student of relationship building, the quote makes me think about relationships and networking on LinkedIn in particular.

LinkedIn networking can be a terrific way to start a relationship!

In the early stages where you have just connected with someone, you can engage with that person on LinkedIn as follows:

- Wish that person a happy birthday, congratulate them on their new job, promotion or work anniversary
- Ask your new connection what kind of article interests them and if you see an article that may be of interest, pass that article to your connection
- Like, comment or share a post that was written by your connection
- Follow up with your connection on a topic that you know is important to them

It takes two to tango, so if someone engages with you on LinkedIn, acknowledge that person and say "thank you."

To take the relationship to the next level, invite your connection to a coffee. Face-to-face meetings are helpful to get to know someone and to see a person's body language. A face-to-face meeting is a way to make more of an impression on someone.

The frequency and quality of communication are important. It's not much of a relationship if you're communicating with someone only once a year. The quality of communication is about what you talk about. Once you have been talking for a while and you have reached a certain level of comfort and trust, you start sharing what's important to you: your hopes, dreams, concerns, fears, etc. At this point the relationship has deepened and what started off as networking on LinkedIn turns into.... (gasp) a friendship!

My Cosmic Journey

I am a Human Resources professional in transition who, as a positive person, develops positive relationships in both personal and professional contexts. I would thrive in a company that supports a positive workplace culture.

My job search feels like I'm on a cosmic journey, hurtling through space where I'm charting unknown territory. I'm meeting terrific people in random and unexpected ways. I don't know what (if anything) will come out of meeting a certain person on a certain day.

In November 2015 I was at a Tuni Talk in Toronto (a networking/speakers event). I attended this Tuni Talk with a friend. I invited my friend along, so that I would feel bolstered to strike up a conversation with people I don't know. I struck up a conversation with a gentleman who was standing alone and engaged on his smartphone. It turned out that we were already a second level connection on LinkedIn as we had a few connections in common. We also share an interest in positive workplace cultures. I consider this person to be my mentor and friend who always provides supportive comments on my LinkedIn posts.

I wonder what the probability was to meet this person? First, I decided to attend this particular Tuni Talk and secondly I decided to approach this person and strike up a conversation. I think meeting this person was a serendipitous encounter!

One of my LinkedIn connections reminded me about the Law of Attraction, i.e., like-minded people will be attracted to you by what you are putting out in the universe. I decided to write a

LinkedIn blog and to put out some positive vibes via my posts. Someone who I didn't know read one of my LinkedIn posts. She must have liked what she read, because she decided to contact me on LinkedIn and offered me a volunteer opportunity. Another example of the Law of Attraction is that there was someone who I met at a different Tuni Talk who later decided to invite me to a coffee networking meeting, primarily, I think, because he liked what I was writing in my posts.

Among my HR peers, we talk about people who have "landed" or found jobs. When I think of "landed" I think of a vessel (like a spaceship) that has reached its destination.

Unfortunately I haven't yet landed and it's this part of the journey that feels uncomfortable, of not knowing if (or when) I will land a job. In the meantime I am enjoying the journey itself and meeting new people and spending time with family and friends.

In this journey of ours we sometimes feel down on ourselves.

Here is what I would like to remind anyone who is on a job search journey like myself:

- Know what you're looking for (Know thyself)
- Keep the faith
- Stay positive
- Believe in yourself
- Enjoy the journey

Gonna Fly Now

I am a Job Seeker in Transition.

I am a Human Resources disruptor at heart. Jacob Morgan is a futurist and author of *The Future of Work*. He advocates for organizations to do things that contribute to the "employee experience" such that employees want to go to work instead of feeling compelled to have to go to work. As an HR professional I would like to work in a tech-like culture where employee experience matters.

I recently read a LinkedIn post by Rakesh Kana and Trang Pham called "Couple job hunt on the streets of Toronto—Click, like, share. And give my family a tomorrow." This is a couple who recently immigrated to Toronto. They have done all the things you're supposed to do to search for a job (network, go online and apply, visit companies, talk to recruiters, etc.) and to no avail. They decided that they would go out and network in the streets of Toronto, be human billboards and hand out résumés. They documented this unorthodox approach to job searching in their LinkedIn post.

I draw inspiration from this post. Aspects of this story reminds me of qualities you would find in a tech-like culture as I describe below.

Collaboration. You'll find collaboration in a tech-like culture. Tech-like cultures include an open physical workspace that encourages employees to mingle and exchange ideas. Being a collaborative person, I would like to try and assist Rakesh and Trang. May I suggest that you follow Ali Moayedi on LinkedIn? Ali is a friend of mine who is a Job Developer at the Centre for

Education and Training. Ali regularly posts positions that he's working on on LinkedIn.

Disruptive (innovative). The part of Rakesh and Trang's story that I find disruptive is posting their innovative job search efforts on LinkedIn. The post has (so far) garnered 293 likes and 63 comments! Rakesh and Trang's post acts like a crowdfunding web site. But, instead of raising money, the post acts as a lightning rod for people to come and offer helpful job search advice! I suppose it takes a village to find a job nowadays!

Fail fast (resiliency). In a tech-like culture, you hear about failing fast, i.e., you don't have to hide your mistakes, but learn from them and move on. I find Rakesh and Trang's resiliency very admirable. They realized that the traditional ways of finding a job weren't working for them, and so they regrouped and tried an innovative approach.

"Gonna Fly Now" is a song from the movie *Rocky* (1976) with Sylvester Stallone. In the movie Rocky was an underdog who in the end triumphed.

My wish is for Rakesh and Trang (and all job seekers) to have their "Rocky" moment and to experience triumph.

I think we deserve it.

With a Little Help from My Friends

Whitney Johnson had a networking initiative where if you were interested, she would randomly pair you up with someone in her network and you could network with that person via Skype. The purpose of the initiative was for two people to help each other. For example, maybe you can help that person by opening up your network and introducing that person to someone in your network.

I volunteered to participate in Ms. Johnson's networking initiative, because as a job seeker I want to meet new people.

What does "networking" mean to me? You become quite practiced in striking up a conversation with people you don't know. I try to connect with people on a personal level. I like to learn something about the person and identify common ground. Maybe I'll ask a question or maybe I can talk about something from my experience that coincides with the conversational flow. After the conversation I'll look for opportunities to engage with that person. Maybe I can share something with them like an event, an article or even one of my posts.

When Ms. Johnson introduced me to someone in her network, I was excited to learn that I'd be Skyping with someone from another country! (I'm from Canada.)

We had our Skype conversation earlier this week. We had a great conversation!

What I appreciated most about the Skype conversation was that the other person was PRESENT. I felt heard. The other person was very patient and waited until I finished my thought. This person was an attentive listener.

I on the other hand, if you're talking to me face-to-face, can become excited and sometimes interrupt. I was very good and did not interrupt once during the conversation! I was very attentive and focused on everything that this person had to say.

During the conversation I mentioned that I was in transition. We talked about why we work. Immediately I said that I would like to work so that I could once again draw an income. My Skype partner then reminded me of some of the other reasons why we work: to feel engaged, to feel that we belong in an organization and to feel a sense of purpose in the work that we're carrying out.

I had no expectations of what this conversation would bring, but I can honestly say that this conversation helped me out. When you have been in transition for a while, you begin to think that finding a job is quite elusive and you forget some of the deeper reasons for why you want to work!

I can't speak to whether the other person felt that I helped, but they did appreciate my perspective on things.

Thank you, Whitney Johnson, for organizing this terrific networking initiative!

I found it very helpful!

Tap Into Passion

I was reading an article by Warren Berger recently called "Find Your Passion With These 8 Thought-Provoking Questions."

One of these questions is finding your sentence. How would you describe what you love to do and to encapsulate this in a sentence?

I came up with my sentence.

I was surprised with what I came up with.

"I love connecting with people (relationship management), connecting people with information (customer service) and mobilizing people (team building)."

Let me explain each element of my sentence.

1. Connecting with people. I look for all kinds of touch points to connect with people. For example, I'll forward an article that may be of interest to them; wish people a "Happy Birthday" and congratulate them on a workplace milestone. When someone sends me an e-mail, this is an opportunity to engage and I return all my e-mails quickly. I love having meaningful face-to-face conversations with people. I like to talk more than surface stuff—what are your hopes and dreams, what are your passions? I like to get to know people.

2. Connecting people with information. I love attending arts and culture events like Doors Open Toronto. So not only do I like attending, but I like to tell people about these events, so that they may consider attending too! For example, I've sent updates on LinkedIn to remind people in my network about this event.

I loved volunteering at Neighbourhood Link. I volunteered in their Employment Resource & Information Centre. I helped job seekers with their online job searches like filling out an online application and showing them how to use the fax machine.

3. Mobilizing people. I love fundraising for the Terry Fox Foundation. I'm really proud that my sponsors and I raised $1,005 for the Foundation in 2016! What I think about is that one donation alone (like $1) doesn't sound very significant, but what if you can mobilize the people in your network, so that 1000 people each donate $1… that's a thousand dollars raised! There's power in the collective when you can mobilize people!

I loved being the Employee Campaign Chair for Combined Insurance's United Way Campaigns. I got the chance to collaborate with colleagues from different departments to plan and execute our campaigns. All of us believed in the United Way, and so all I needed to do was to mobilize our efforts.

As part of my love for connecting with people, I love to discover what their passions are.

I learned early on from a friend of mine that he loves backgammon. When I was 18, I received a backgammon set for a birthday present. I never opened that set until recently, because it was too daunting for me to learn backgammon!

I love to play cribbage. I don't know too many people in my network who play cribbage, but I like to play.

I suggested to my friend that if he teaches me how to play backgammon, I would teach him how to play cribbage.

I now know how to play backgammon and I have a cribbage partner.

If we take the time to learn what another person's passions are, we open up the possibility for ourselves to learn something new, to share what we know and deepen our connections with others.

What is a passion of yours that you would like to share with the world?

Time Travel

I bumped into a high school classmate of mine. He was doing his run and I was out for a walk, and our paths happened to meet.

The other day I invited my former high school classmate to a coffee.

We talked for 3½ hours at the coffee. It was amazing to learn about all the sports he's participated in. To this day he still runs and skis. When he was younger he thought wouldn't it be cool to try parachuting. Instead of just thinking about doing it, he actually went and did it. He's travelled to places where he could run or ski. He epitomizes the word "adventurous."

We got to talking about our old school days.

Back in the day I always knew him to say "hello" in the halls but that was about it.

He told me that we were in the same math class and that he sat behind me!

He told me that he had difficulty with that math class and that I tried to help him!

Eventually he dropped out of the math class. He made up for the math class by attending an extra semester somewhere else.

Our paths never did meet after we finished high school.

It was just recently that we met and only by accident.

I remarked that we have come full circle: We grew up together. We drifted apart. We reconnected.

I'm amazed that he remembered where we sat in math class. I'm glad to know that I tried to help him. Even from a young age I was trying to help people!

He remarked that we were in different academic streams, that I was in the stream for "smart" students.

I never thought of myself as being smarter than other people. In fact I've come to realize that I have something to learn from everyone I meet.

It's a fact of life that my high school classmate and I ran in different social circles.

We never really knew each other.

Now that we've grown up, we can if we want get to know each other and become friends.

I think I'll invite him out for another coffee.

Positive Vibes

People recognize a vibe about you faster than you realize it about yourself.

A couple of years ago a LinkedIn connection commented that I had a "nice smile."

If you asked me then, I would say that that was a nice compliment.

Ask me now what that compliment means to me, and I would say that it's a pretty good indication of who I am.

I've always been a positive person.

People in the past called me "smiley" or commented that I'm "optimistic."

Does that mean I'm happy?

No, I'm not happy all the time.

But I'm always positive.

We can do things to put ourselves in a more positive state of mind.

Lately to put myself in a more positive state of mind, I journal, go for a walk and meet friends.

I am a job seeker in transition.

Yesterday I had the opportunity to make someone's day.

I went to see my barber for a haircut.

During the course of our conversation, my barber noted that he was experiencing discomfort because he has arthritis. His doctor prescribed pills to manage the pain, but offered no other advice.

I suggested to my barber that he check into the Arthritis Society web site (arthritis.ca), because there would be resources for him to check out.

I went home and I thought to myself that although my barber said he would check out the web site, he probably wouldn't.

I signed on to my computer and proceeded to go to the Arthritis Society web site and printed pages for my barber to read. I made sure that I printed the contact information for the Arthritis Society.

I went back to my barber and handed him the pages that I printed.

My barber thanked me and said that he will call the Arthritis Society. I believe he will call.

We can lift our own moods when we help someone out.

I felt happy that I connected my barber to the Arthritis Society.

Sometimes we help ourselves when we help someone else.

Have you heard Elton John's song "Sad Songs" that was released in 1984?

It's an upbeat song that will give you a positive vibe!

Positivity… Let Me Count the Ways

In a previous post, I mentioned to job seekers to "stay hopeful and positive."

I would like to expand on how exactly job seekers (or anyone else for that matter) can "stay positive."

First I'm reminded of a FISH! Philosophy tenet of "Choose Your Attitude."

We can choose to have a positive attitude in a number of ways.

Be nice to yourself

We can't always feel positive (or up or cheery) all of the time. Sometimes we feel down. I suggest that we accept that we feel down at this moment and that this feeling won't last forever. We can think to ourselves that things will feel brighter tomorrow. Give yourself permission to feel down at this moment and take comfort that tomorrow is another day.

We can do some basic things to take care of ourselves: get enough rest, drink lots of water, eat healthy, get some exercise, etc. Other than these things, we can participate in activities that make us happy. For me, it's spending time with family and friends.

It may be helpful to keep a gratitude journal. For me, it's reflecting what I find to be a positive experience every day. We are prone to always seeing the negative, but if we train ourselves to see the positives, we become open to seeing and embracing new possibilities.

Be nice to others

Words matter and what we say to people. We can "Make Someone's Day" (another FISH! Philosophy tenet) just in the way we interact with them. We all know that if we treat someone badly, that can have a negative viral effect. Similarly, if we are nice to people, that too has a viral effect, but this time it's a positive viral effect! As one of my friends says, it always pays to pay it forward!

We can perceive situations differently

We can adapt our thinking to think in a more positive light. For example, it's a grey day. We can think it's not the most nicest of days; however, if you are a walker like I am, you can also think to yourself that you can step out of the house without having to spend time putting on sunscreen and a hat! There is more than one way to look at a situation.

Our negative self-talk can limit us; however, we can push beyond our fear and go beyond our comfort zone and take comfort in having conquered a fear. I think about a quote that is currently on a friend's LinkedIn profile: "Everything you've ever wanted is on the other side of fear."

We can alter our perception on how we think people are treating us

You say "hello" to a colleague in the hallway and they don't say "hello" back. We may think that our colleague is ignoring us or that they're being "stuck-up." But if we gave this person the benefit of the doubt, we could also think that that person is distracted and thinking about something else, or maybe that person didn't hear us. It's not always all about us.

Let me end by sharing a song by Sara Bareilles called "Brave."

It's an upbeat song with a positive message!

Try

Like you, I was a job searcher up until three weeks ago.

I have a lot of empathy for the situation you find yourself in.

It's important to acknowledge your disappointment and other feelings you may be feeling.

But after that it's time to try to move on, even a little bit.

You may not like (or possibly hear) the suggestions that I make about possible jobs to look into.

But maybe you can file my suggestions away and look at them again when you're ready to explore some new possibilities?

I know it may be hard to believe, but there are people who want to help you.

In Ontario there are government-funded agencies that will help you in your job search.

Ask for informational interviews.

Tap into your LinkedIn network for advice and support.

If we are connected, I would love to help, if only to provide suggestions.

Try to find some inspiration to think a little more positively.

For me, I find inspiration in Pink's song "Try", particularly this line:

"You gotta get up and try, and try, and try"

Maybe think of a quote that you find inspiring.

I heard Tim Cork give a speech a couple of years ago.

In that speech he said this quote that I find inspirational:

"The past is history, the future is a mystery, today is a gift that is called the present"

We don't have control over what people think, but we do have control over our own thoughts, feelings and perceptions.

It's important to manage the impressions that others form of us.

How are you coming across in interviews?

Are you coming across as a positive person who can help with an employer's pain?

Or are you holding on to perceptions about how others may have treated you in the past?

I came across a Forbes article today called "How workers in their 50s and 60s can thrive in today's fast-changing world."

Notwithstanding the headline, this article is of interest to all job seekers, whatever your age.

The article suggests that job seekers seek to continuously learn, be open to change and to reinventing themselves.

I know it's difficult, but when you're ready, try to set aside the past and think a little more positively.

Reflect on your skills and what you like to do.

Be open to learning and thinking about how you can apply your skills in this fast-changing world of ours.

My friend once said to me "maintain the persistence."

And I for one know you can do it.

Taking Stock

I had the opportunity to present to a group of job seekers.

I wasn't sure how they wanted to be addressed, but we landed on "mature workers."

Personally I like to treat people as they are and not group anyone in a particular generational category.

We all have particular strengths.

Your strengths are best suited for some situations and my strengths are best suited to other situations.

We complement each other.

When you are a job seeker, we tend to "know" what our strengths are.

But for me, I was feeling stuck.

I was applying to human resources jobs (what I know best) and not getting the intended results.

I need to disrupt myself.

I learned recently about doing a skills inventory where you reflect and write down the transferable skills that you have.

I think this can go further.

Let's call this an Inventory of You.

The categories are fluid, but here are some to start off with.

Skills—What are the skills that you have acquired from your work and volunteer experiences? Think about particular experiences that makes you think that you have that particular skill. When you can relate a skill to a particular experience, that can help you answer behavioural questions in an interview (Situation Action Result). The skills that you generate from this exercise can be used in the Skills Endorsements section on your LinkedIn profile.

Knowledge—What industries have you worked in that would give you knowledge about that industry (terms, concepts, methods, processes, etc.)?

Credentials—What credentials do you have from formal learning experiences (certificates, diplomas, degrees, certifications)? Reflect on what those learning experiences mean to you.

Interests—What do you most like to learn about or do in your spare time? Maybe the cooking skills that you excel at could be turned into a catering business?

Mindset—What descriptors describe you best? (I'd use the following descriptors to describe myself: positive, servant's mentality, curious, collaborative.)

Values—What do you value at this time? (For me, it's spending time with family and friends. Doing meaningful work.)

Preferences—Which location of the city would you like to work? Do you mind working on the evening shift or on weekends?

When you're in a job search for a long time, you begin to think that you're nothing special, that you're just like everyone else.

But if you do this Inventory of You, you will soon see that no one else has all the skills, interests, values, etc. that you have.

Maybe you can see a pattern and identify a new occupational interest that you can see yourself pursuing thereby reinventing yourself in the process?

"Today you are You, that is truer than true. There is no one alive who is Youer than You." —Dr. Seuss

I referred to Marge Watters's *It's Your Move*, 3rd Edition (2007) in writing this post.

Pearls of Wisdom

Every day I say some quotes to myself that I find affirming.

Maybe you might like some of these quotes as well!

1. Winnie-the-Pooh (A.A. Milne)

"It is more fun to talk with someone who doesn't use long difficult words, but rather short easy words like 'What about lunch?'" —A.A. Milne

I think of one of my friends in particular who is very unpretentious and easy-going. I aspire to be like him.

2. Winnie-the-Pooh (A.A. Milne)

"You can't stay in your corner of the forest waiting for others to come to you. You have to go to them sometimes." —A. A. Milne

Sometimes you just have to take the initiative. Is there a friend who you haven't seen in a while? If so, invite them out to a coffee!

3. Winnie-the-Pooh (A.A. Milne)

"You are braver than you believe, stronger than you seem and smarter than you think." —A.A. Milne

I know that as a job seeker, I felt that I lost my way. Maybe this quote will give all job seekers a boost of confidence.

4. Dr. Seuss

"Be who you are and say what you feel, because those who mind don't matter and those who matter don't mind." —Dr. Seuss (attributed)

I think that being authentic is the way to go.

5. Dr. Seuss

> "Why fit in when you were born to stand out?"
> —Dr. Seuss (attributed)

Again, being authentic is the way to go.

6. Dr. Seuss

> "The more that you read, the more things you will know. The more that you learn, the more places you'll go." —Dr. Seuss

Continuous learning is key. We can learn a lot from reading!

7. Dr. Seuss

> "You have brains in your head. You have feet in your shoes. You can steer yourself any direction you choose." —Dr. Seuss

We can choose our attitude.

A.A. Milne and Dr. Seuss wrote children's books; however, I didn't read either of these authors as a child. I've only recently been reading and mulling over their quotes. I suppose you can say that both these authors' works are timeless!

I never think it's a good idea to be who you think others expect you or want you to be. Being yourself is the best way to go.

> "Be yourself, everyone else is already taken." —Oscar Wilde (attributed)

Happy New Year Everyone!

Launch

I invite you to the launch of my new blog web site on the Blogger platform!

I call my blog "The Positive Pathfinder."

You can find my blog at thepositivepathfinder.blogspot.com.

I wanted to expand my social media presence. I wanted to learn something new. And I wanted to set up a portfolio of my posts where I could direct potential employers to.

After pondering 72 names over 2 days, I decided on calling my blog "The Positive Pathfinder."

First I'm a positive guy.

Also, I'm at a stage in life where I feel like I'm in flux. Don't quite know what I'll be doing, but I know I want to pursue some interests of mine, like setting up a blog web site (done) and taking an improv class (done and in progress).

I am positive that I am not the only one who feels like they are in flux and so I am excited to continue to share my thoughts and experiences with you and to draw inspiration from your thoughts and experiences as well. We can learn and inspire each other!

I started my LinkedIn blog on December 12, 2015. My Blogger web site starts today, January 13, 2017.

I recreated many of my LinkedIn posts onto the Blogger platform. I was diligent in checking that all the links in my

Blogger posts were working and that paragraph breaks were the same.

Starting today I will post my posts in both the LinkedIn and Blogger platforms.

In the Blogger platform I grouped my posts into categories, which I've named:

Experiential

Inspirational

Joy or Wonder

Mindset or Skillset

Reflective

You can share my Blogger posts on other platforms and subscribe to my posts via e-mail.

I would like to explore new interests this year and this initiative is representative of this desire.

"Don't ask yourself what the world needs. Ask yourself what make makes you come alive and then go do that. Because what the world needs is people who have come alive." —Howard Thurman

Walking Zombie

I was a walking zombie when I worked at Combined Insurance.

It's not that I was slacking off and not doing my work.

It was quite the opposite.

All I did was think about work.

I'd stay late every day and take work home with me on the weekends.

I fell into a routine.

And (not so) suddenly I lost my job.

And in my transition during the last 4 years, I've taken on a new attitude.

While work is important to me, I am actively pursuing other interests.

Just recently I starting taking improv classes, which are finishing up in two weeks time.

I've signed up to take a Mental Health First Aid Course in April 2017.

I keep a to-do list of things that I want to do in the future because they are personally satisfying to me.

I am thinking that if I follow my passions that I might be able to identify a path to follow when I look for my next opportunity.

I love getting together with friends.

I am interested to hear about their passions and what projects they are working on.

Their stories inspire me to follow my passions.

Or sometimes to follow theirs.

It broadens your horizons when you talk to your friends.

I've become a bit more adventurous lately.

I will try something that I haven't tried before.

Recently I tried a new cuisine.

I was avoiding this cuisine because my "delicate" constitution can't take spicy food anymore.

I'm glad to have tried the food, but even their most "blandest" of foods was still a little spicy for me.

I was adventurous enough to give it a try.

I've become an open person.

I don't mind talking about myself, being "out there" and making myself vulnerable.

I'll say "I don't know" if I don't know something.

I've become much more open to feedback.

I appreciate friends' feedback and while I may not act on their feedback right away, I will file the feedback in my mind and revisit the feedback in the future if that becomes appropriate.

I like Katy Perry's new song "Chained to the Rhythm" that she sang at the 2017 Grammys.

One of the reasons I like this song is that she includes the phrase "wasted zombie" in her lyrics.

I don't think that I'll ever go back to being a walking zombie.

I'm a much more freer person and say what I want to say (respectfully, of course).

I like to spend time with friends and family and that to me is a priority.

I pursue my interests and hopefully some of my interests will intersect with what I get to do at work.

I suppose you can say that I want to enjoy life a little more.

I may ask you: "What project will you be working on next?"

Some time goes by and I'll ask about your progress.

And when you reach your goal I get excited for you and I congratulate you on your win.

The Personal Touch

I read an article today called "How to Connect With An Aging Parent" by David Maxfield.

As I was reading the article, the things that this article talks about applies to connecting with ANYBODY.

The article is set up like an advice column. A reader wrote in to say that when her husband talks to his mother about current events, his mother seems to get very categorical. Mr. Maxfield suggests that the husband change the topic of conversation and make it more personal when he talks to his mother.

Mr. Maxfield suggested some ways to make the conversation more "personal."

Inclusivity. Mr. Maxfield suggested that the husband call his mother every day, so that she feels more included in his life.

When I was chairing committee meetings at Combined Insurance and I was telling something to the committee, I would make sure that I made eye contact (briefly) with each and every person. I wanted to make sure that they felt included. If I'm at a networking event and I'm talking to two people, I make sure that I shift eye contact from one person to the next and back to the other person, etc. and not focus my attention entirely on one person. The other person who I'm not making eye contact with is going to feel excluded.

At Combined Insurance, when an employee dropped into the HR office, I'd drop what I was doing, got up from my seat, go over and talk to the employee and make eye contact. There's nothing worse than having to talk to someone when they're busily engaged doing something else. You feel ignored. I focused my attention on the employee with the intention of making that person feel that they were the most important person in the world in that moment.

Shift the spotlight to the other person. Mr. Maxfield suggested that the husband ask his mother questions that gets her to talk about herself, and this shows the husband's interest in his mother.

At a networking event you introduce yourself to different people. I'm always conscious about not wanting to talk about myself for too long. Once I sense that I've talked about myself for long enough, I switch the focus and ask about the other person. You need to give and take in any situation. In a networking situation, you are "giving" by showing an interest in the other person by asking questions and listening to what they say. You are "taking" by talking about yourself and asking them to focus their attention on you.

Shared experience. Mr. Maxfield suggests that the husband find a TV show that both he and his mother enjoy. Watching the same show creates an experience that they can talk about later and they can relive the joy.

A networking experience where you meet face to face is the best. For example, I checked in recently with a LinkedIn connection who I hadn't "talked to" in a while. I sent her a short note and attached one of my posts. She said that she remembers when we met at a networking event. After the event we discovered we were going in the same direction on the subway and so we shared a subway ride and had a nice, long talk! We had a few minutes to talk at the networking event, but the subway ride was memorable, because it was an opportunity to have a more in-depth talk.

One time I attended a virtual networking event. After the event I connected with two people on LinkedIn. Since then I've swapped a few messages with one of these people, but a virtual networking event isn't quite as memorable.

There are so many ways to make someone feel special.

You can make eye contact when you're talking with someone.

You can ask someone questions and show your interest in them.

You can create a "special" moment by taking the time to have a face-to-face conversation with someone and recounting the experience with them at a later time.

The headline "How to Connect With An Aging Parent" intrigued me.

I expected to learn a secret about connecting with people.

But instead they talk about things that I do all along.

It's all about doing things that make people feel special.

And giving each person you meet —

The Personal Touch.

Elevator Pitch

My friend George Khalife shared an elevator story with his network this week.

George stepped into an elevator. He was listening to music on personal earbuds (or headphones). A fellow elevator passenger noticed the blazer he was wearing and remarked: "Love that blazer! What does the symbol mean?" George removed his earbuds in anticipation of a conversation and replied: "Thanks! Not sure to be honest, but it looks cool." This initial exchange was followed up with an introduction of names, where they work, an exchange of business cards and the possibility for future networking!

When I read George's update on LinkedIn, I had a feeling that I may have experienced my elevator story on or about the same day that George shared his elevator story.

Last Tuesday it was the end of the day and the elevator stopped on the 4th floor where I work. I stepped into the elevator. A gentleman was already in the elevator from an upper floor. I could tell he wanted to say something (he was shooting me glances) and finally asked me if I worked in the same building to which I said yes. That began a conversation as to where we work, what we do, ethnic origin (!) and an exchange of business cards.

I found out from my new acquaintance that he is in retirement planning. I am bolder than I have ever been before and I asked him if he sold products that were specific to a particular financial institution—he explained no, that wasn't the case. When we arrived on the 1st floor, I showed him our agency's name on the directory, as he may not have heard where I was working.

We connected on LinkedIn.

I didn't initiate the conversation in the elevator, but another time I did.

It was April 11, the day of the Toronto Blue Jays home opener. I was coming home from work on the subway. I was in an especially happy mood because it was a special day for Toronto Blue Jays fans. I noticed Jays fans at the Wilson subway station and Warden subway station. I asked both times if they were going to the game and both times they answered "yes." I wished them a good time at the game.

I was curious about whether some Jays fans were going to a game, and so I just asked them. I had the courage to strike up a conversation.

You can network anywhere and anytime.

You don't necessarily have to wait for an opening to talk to people.

Sometimes you can create a networking opportunity all on your own.

Flourish

I get to organize free educational meet-ups at the Ontario Society of Senior Citizens Organizations.

The intended audience are unemployed job seekers who are either 50+ or a newcomer to Canada.

The meet-ups are an opportunity for attendees to come to our office (in Toronto) to network and to learn an idea or two from our invited speakers.

Our first meet-up was on February 28, 2017.

At the time our way to get the word out about our meet-ups was to pick up the phone and to personally reach out to community agencies.

I'd say, "Would you be open to distributing our poster to your network?"

I'd follow up with an e-mail and attach our poster.

Some community agencies responded with a non-response.

Some community agencies wrote back to say that they distributed our poster to their network.

Some community agencies were open to engaging in a phone conversation.

Since February 28, we've held meet-ups on March 10, April 20 and May 12th with future meet-ups scheduled on May 18th, May 25, June 8 and June 13.

When I first started to contact community agencies, I thought it was a futile exercise.

One of my colleagues said to me that I was planting a seed for the future.

And she was right.

As registrants called to register, I'd ask where they learned about our meet-ups.

I'd learn that participants were learning about our meet-ups from the agencies where I was sending our posters to.

I was starting to see the fruit of my labours, because our posters were getting noticed by our intended audience.

My outreach to community agencies was a form of networking.

At first I wasn't seeing any results.

As time went by I realized that I needed to be patient and let things unfold as they may.

To network is to plant a seed.

And with a little luck and (loving) care, things will flourish!

Wonder Story

At work we have been organizing a series of educational meet-ups.

All 6 of us pitch in with these meet-ups.

My task was to arrange speakers.

I wondered how I was going to bring in speakers.

One day in 2016, I was looking at my LinkedIn feed and found Rakesh Kana's story of how he and his wife (both newcomers to Canada) were having a difficult time finding a job. They were using all the traditional methods that you can think of to find a job, but to no avail. They decided to take a novel approach to their job search by wearing sandwich boards and handing out their résumés to passersby while standing in front of Union Station in Toronto. They were successful in landing jobs.

Rakesh wrote a LinkedIn post about his and his wife's job search experiences. You can read their post here.

I was inspired by Rakesh's post and I wrote a post that referenced them.

Flash forward a couple of weeks ago.

I messaged Rakesh on LinkedIn to see if he would be interested in presenting a talk at one of our educational meet-ups. I hadn't talked to Rakesh in awhile, I wasn't even sure if he would remember me, and to my amazement he said "yes" to coming and presenting a talk! We had a telephone conversation to make arrangements. Yesterday I had the pleasure of meeting Rakesh!

By June 13th we will have had 13 speakers at these educational meet-ups.

I knew 4 of these speakers prior to my asking them. I met all 4 at networking events where someone had to strike up a conversation with the other.

Amazingly I hadn't met the other 9 speakers before their presentations! Some of these speakers were referrals. Some of these speakers I had connected with on LinkedIn and we messaged from time to time.

One day my manager and I were listening to a webinar. We both thought that one of the webinar presenters would be a fitting speaker to speak at an educational meet-up. I contacted the webinar presenter by phone about coming to speak and amazingly she agreed!

It goes to show you that you can network on LinkedIn or by phone or in person.

I was lucky enough to be able to leverage my network and find speakers for our meet-ups!

Sometimes all you need to do is to ask.

But remember to give in return.

I suppose what goes around, comes around.

Curious Story

"Curiosity" seems to be popping up all around me.

Recently one of my LinkedIn connections, Michael Zeidenberg, posted these thoughts about curiosity:

> "Saturday's thought: They say, curiosity kills the cat. But, I believe taking the time during the day and to focus on being curious about people, events and ideas will only lead us to greater personal growth. Besides, you never know what conversations will lead to learning something new, a new friendship, a new job, or a business adventure. Cheers to embracing the concept of curiosity as its good for the soul!"
> —Michael Zeidenberg

At work we organized an educational meet-up for job seekers called "Curiosity is the secret weapon for job seekers 50+."

I know that it's not obvious from the topic headline as to what this meet-up was going to be about.

I gather that people who came to our meet-up were curious.

Some of our meet-up attendees were newcomers and some of our meet-up attendees were older.

By being curious and attending this meet-up, each attendee was reminded (by other attendees) about a perspective that they might not have been aware of.

"Some older job seekers experience a barrier of ageism."

"Some newcomers experience a barrier of not having Canadian experience."

As Michael Zeidenberg indicated about being curious: "...you never know what conversations will lead to learning something new..."

I recently connected on LinkedIn to someone I had not met before.

For both the sender and me, I think we were both curious as to where the LinkedIn connection could lead.

Sometimes you connect with someone on LinkedIn and a connection lays dormant.

And a relationship doesn't have a chance to take off.

But as Michael Zeidenberg indicated about being curious: "you never know what conversations will lead to... a new friendship."

The latter happened to me when I connected on LinkedIn to the person I had not met before.

Nik Beeson was one of our presenters at our educational meet-up.

My take-away from Nik's presentation was that there is a link between stress and curiosity.

When we are stressed, we are worried about something and we focus on that worry.

Being curious and open to possibilities fall to the wayside.

If we can reduce our stress and engage in a reflective activity like going for a walk, journalling, painting, meditation, yoga, etc., we open ourselves up to being curious and seeing possibilities.

I do things to reduce stress.

Maybe that's why I've been noticing "curiosity" all around me.

Storybook Life

I've been thinking about "stories" lately.

I named my last two posts "Curious Story" and "Wonder Story" and now this, "Storybook Life."

Everyone has a story to tell.

And everyone has an interesting story.

At work we asked people to fill out an "intake questionnaire" for a project they participated in called "Enhancing Economic Opportunities for Older Workers 50–70."

I don't know all the people who participated in the project, but I find myself trying to create a narrative (story) about the "typical" person who participated in the project. I have a lot of empathy for everyone who participated in our project—they don't have an easy life.

In "real" life I like to arrange coffee meet-ups with friends. We share stories. We tell something about ourselves. I learn something new about them every time. With each story told, I am getting to know them. Each of us has an evolving story.

I have online relationships with friends. We regularly send short messages to each other on e-mail or LinkedIn. This too is an evolving story. With every passing message I learn a little bit more about them.

For some people, their stories have ended.

Someone who I used to go to coffee meet-ups with disappeared from my network and no longer returns messages. I don't think of how our story ended, but instead think about the fun times we had at those meet-ups.

We recently had a death in my family (aunt). I'm not sure if I really knew my aunt, but I will remember the times we'd gather as a family for a special occasion like a birthday or Chinese New Year. All of those occasions add up to a lifetime of memories.

Sometimes you don't even need to meet a person to enjoy hearing their stories.

I subscribe to Brian Rashid's and Whitney Johnson's newsletters.

I look forward to seeing their e-mails in my inbox, opening their e-mails and reading their stories.

The most important story is our own story.

It's funny that for everyone we meet, we fill in missing information and come up with a narrative for that person. We should do the same for ourselves, reflect and understand our own personal story. For example, what do we value, what do we stand for and how do we want to show up for people?

What is your story?

I love to hear personal stories.

Different

Ann DeLuca is a Coach. She came to the Ontario Society of Senior Citizens Organizations (OSSCO) on June 13th and conducted a workshop called "Getting Clear on What's Next." Everyone (including me) was in transition. We were invited to come with an open mind and try some new and different exercises (like visualization exercises). I was reminded that it's good to be in a relaxed state of mind to help identify possibilities for ourselves. When we're stressed we focus on the stress and less on seeing possibilities. As I mentioned in an earlier post, we can engage in reflective activities to help put us in a relaxed state of mind like yoga, meditation, walking, painting, writing, etc. I realized that seeking the services of a coach could be an option to pursue.

Rakesh Kana tried something different in his job search. When traditional job search methods weren't producing the desired result, he and his wife tried something new by putting on sandwich boards and handing out their résumés (in a pen) to passersby at Union Station. They found jobs using this novel approach.

While working at OSSCO, I came across job seekers who were reluctant to post their profiles on LinkedIn. Using LinkedIn is a way to help job seekers to stand out, but I understand that everyone has their own reasons to do (or not to do) something.

Sometimes you just don't want to stand out and to be perceived as different.

For example, I don't have a smartphone. I think wouldn't it be wonderful to be like everyone else and own a smartphone? I have my reasons (like cost). I am able to work around it. For example, I rely on my friend (who has a smartphone) to take pictures and preserve the memories of a shared experience like attending Nuit Blanche.

I get it that (sometimes) we don't want to do something because we don't want to be perceived as different.

I challenge you to be a little different.

If there is something new that you haven't done before and you are considering doing that something "new," that is being different.

I'll celebrate with you for doing that something "new" that is new to you and going beyond your comfort zone.

I like this Albert Einstein quote that I recently saw on LinkedIn:

"Insanity: doing the same thing over and over again and expecting different results."

It's OK to be different.

Job Search Chronicles

Last Friday I completed Plum.io's free online Talent Assessment. You receive feedback immediately about your Top 3 Talents. I learned that I had a talent that I wasn't aware that I had!

The following day I met up with a friend for a coffee at the mall.

I showed my Talents profile to my friend.

My friend was very encouraging. He suggested that I could attach my Talents profile to my application when I apply for a job.

When you complete the Talent Assessment, Plum.io suggests that you could share your profile on social media.

I combined my friend's and Plum.io's ideas and came up with something that I haven't done before.

I decided to send the following message and attach my Talents profile to select members of my LinkedIn network.

"I share my Talents Profile with you (via Plum.io) and let you know that I'm looking for a part-time role in HR or job search mentoring in Toronto!"

This message was a "touching base" e-mail. I wanted to let my network know what I was doing and what I was looking for.

I wanted to encourage a conversation. One of my friends wanted to know what Plum.io was. Another friend wanted to know why I was sending this message. A couple of friends told me that they will keep their eyes open for possible opportunities.

Lessons Learned

- So much of job searching is planting a seed. I wanted to plant a seed and let friends know that I am looking for a job and what in particular I am looking for. If they come across a job opening in the future that I might be suited for, perhaps they will think of me.
- It really is important to network. If I hadn't met up with my friend at the mall, I wouldn't have been encouraged to share my Talents profile. You gain new ideas when you talk to people. You might even become inspired to try something new!
- I was impressed with the Plum Talent Assessment, because the 3 Talents that it identified for me is very accurate. Plum.io has done a great thing to help job seekers to identify their talents. Plum.io's Talent Assessment tool may be helpful to employers in identifying qualified candidates quickly and in moving a recruitment process along a little faster!

All in all I had a good day today in my job search because I had an opportunity to network with friends on LinkedIn.

Job Search Chronicles, Continued

Last Monday I attempted to reconnect (via e-mail) with 75 members of my LinkedIn network, first to let them know that I was looking for a job and second to let them know what kind of job I was looking for. I attached my Talents profile (from Plum.io) as an added incentive to look at my e-mail.

One of my friends e-mailed back to sympathize that I have to go through a job search again and that it must be frustrating to have to repeat the process.

I was challenged (in a good way) by this response.

Yes, I definitely have my ups and downs during this job search, but I don't want to be known as a frustrated job searcher.

Instead I would like to be known as an optimistic job searcher.

As a result of my campaign to reconnect with members of my LinkedIn network, I received over 25 responses.

Friends gave me a "thumbs-up" or "thanks for sharing" or "I'll keep my eyes open for you." I appreciate everyone's responses one and all!

Four in particular I'll share with you.

One of my friends asked me to send her my résumé. She said that she will take my CV and Talents profile and pass them to her HR department. I appreciate this WOW of a gesture. I didn't ask her to do this, but she offered anyway.

Another friend said for me to give him a shout if he can help. This friend is a no-nonsense type of guy. He writes in a spare kind of way and says what he means. I appreciate the gesture.

A recruiter friend of mine called me. We have great rapport. We have a common interest in the Toronto Blue Jays. I appreciate the phone call.

Another recruiter friend of mine asked me to send him my résumé. I appreciate the gesture.

I've been thinking about "networking" because of my recent experiences with networking.

Here are my tips about networking:

Tip #1. **Reach out to your network.** A job search feels like a grind. Sometimes we need to notice the small (but good) things that come our way and to appreciate those things. I feel happier just thinking of the nice things that people sent my way in the past few days.

Tip #2. **Form a sounding board.** We all need a sounding board. A friend of mine is also in job search mode. I love helping my friend. I was an HR recruiter for 20+ years and I can share my recruitment experiences with him. We can "talk turkey" about our job searches. I like learning new things from him.

Tip #3. **Expand your network.** I listened to Eric Barker's webinar today called "How to network effectively and create genuine connections." Mr. Barker said that you and your friends will probably know the same things, but to learn new things (like new information or a job lead), you need to expand your network.

Have you thought about reconnecting with someone or expanding your network?

Yoga Story

When I was at university, I checked out the array of activities that I could participate in like ballroom dancing, squash, yoga and fencing.

I never did the fencing, but while at university I took ballroom dancing lessons. I have since hung up my dancing shoes, but I do enjoy watching "Dancing with the Stars."

Years after I left university, I kept up my Hart House membership and I took squash lessons. Squash is fun and I played squash a couple of times.

I recently read a terrific article by Kendra Wright called "4 Things I Learned by Stepping Out of My Comfort Zone 850 Times in a Row." This is an inspirational article. Ms. Wright did something cool by doing 850 things that made her step out of her comfort zone. At the end of Ms. Wright's article, check out the list that she compiled of 100 things that you could do to step out of your comfort zone.

After looking over the list, I immediately thought to myself that I need to do something that I had put off doing for decades, and that was to take a yoga class!

I went online to look at where I could take such a class. I wanted to take a class right away, somewhere close to home and not too expensive. I decided to take a Yin Yang yoga class at the Roots Yoga Studio.

Taking a yoga class was stepping out of my comfort zone primarily because I thought to myself that I didn't want to look like a complete "doofus" in class!

This morning I arrived to class before the door to the studio was even open. A fellow student was already waiting. We struck up a conversation. I was happy to share that it was my first time doing yoga. My new acquaintance is an experienced student of yoga. It was nice to talk to this person who helped calm my nerves. As luck would have it, I found out that we both have an interest in technology. It goes to show you that you can network anywhere, even at a yoga class!

I met the yoga studio receptionist and the instructor both of whom were great! The instructor was very encouraging. At the end of the yoga lesson, the instructor suggested that I might consider taking hatha yoga or restorative yoga. He even teaches a course called "Yoga for Guys"!

The yoga class was a great experience. I learned that I had muscles that I didn't know I had! Some of the poses I knew that I couldn't do and so I didn't do them. I didn't feel like a doofus at all. Everyone was focused on the instructor and followed his lead.

Lessons learned from my yoga class:

1. You can network anywhere, even at a yoga class.
2. Give yourself a gift and do something that takes you out of your comfort zone. You feel a glow of positivity about yourself for having undergone the experience.
3. You have an interesting experience to tell your friends. And maybe your friends might be inspired to follow your lead and do what you did!

I am a job seeker.

We tend to think about things that we have no control over. When we step out of our comfort zones, we are being proactive and creating a feeling of positivity for ourselves.

Have you stepped out of your comfort zone lately?

Ubiquitous Networker

I am a ubiquitous networker.

I look at LinkedIn as soon as I get up in the morning.

Yesterday morning at 6:30 a.m. a friend of mine ("John") sent me a LinkedIn message.

He said that there's a tech job fair at the MaRS Discovery District and that it started at 12 noon.

I thought to myself that I didn't have anything planned, and so I said "yes" to the job fair.

My friend was being very prescient when he said that I could write a post about my job fair experience.

And that the theme could be on how I stepped out of my comfort zone.

When I arrived at the job fair, I surveyed the companies that were there.

I headed straight to a particular booth, because another friend ("Tom") recently applied for a job at that company.

I followed up on Tom's behalf.

I went up to four other booths and introduced myself.

"Hi, my name is Jamie. I'm an HR professional. I'm looking to work at a company as a culture specialist. It could be part-time or contract. Do you already have a culture specialist? Is workplace culture something that your company thinks about?..."

I had no problem in stepping forward, shaking hands and introducing myself.

I visited 5 booths. Representatives from 4 of the booths were polite and attentive. They made my day. A representative from the 5th booth seemed distant. Her advice seemed quite perfunctory when she advised to check back on their web site sometime.

As soon as I got home, I sent out LinkedIn invitations to some of the people that I met. Three people LinkedIn with me. Emotionally I felt exhilarated from stepping out of my comfort zone and striking up conversations with people I didn't know. Adrenaline was pumping through me throughout the evening. I felt exhausted at the end of the evening.

Striking up a conversation is like yin and yang.

Exhilarating and exhausting.

And oh so worthwhile.

Works of Beauty

My friend and I went on an outing to the Butterfly Conservatory in Niagara Falls yesterday.

2000 live butterflies call this place home.

You experience butterflies in a natural setting amongst a backdrop of lush greenery, a gentle waterfall and moist temps.

Earlier this year I attended an art exhibition at the Art Gallery of Ontario called Mystical Landscapes: Masterpieces from Monet, Van Gogh and More.

It seems to me that the Butterfly Conservatory shares certain similarities with an art exhibition.

They both feature works of beauty. The butterflies are beautiful and colourful. They are natural works of beauty. They are like living art. I stood mesmerized looking at the butterflies for an hour and a half.

Several paintings at Mystical Landscapes were enthralling. One painting in particular that I enjoyed was Van Gogh's "Starry Night Over the Rhone." I stood mesmerized looking at this painting for minutes on end. I marvelled at how Van Gogh depicted the reflection of twinkling stars over water at night. Van Gogh's painting is a man-made work of beauty.

Both places attract a respectful crowd. In a video, visitors to the Butterfly Conservatory were cautioned to watch their step in case they were to inadvertently step on a butterfly. Butterflies are delicate creatures. Visitors were advised that if they wanted to move a butterfly in their pathway, that they offer their finger rather than picking up a butterfly by their wings. An orange butterfly parked itself on my friend's finger. Butterflies are gentle creatures. My friend got up close and personal with this butterfly and took a picture on his smartphone just inches away from this butterfly. A grey butterfly parked itself on my blue-checkered shirt. I was so thrilled to have a butterfly visit me that I didn't move for several minutes so that I wouldn't disturb the butterfly. Everyone was so respectful and no one batted at the butterflies! At Mystical Landscapes, everyone was respectful as well. No pushing and shoving. Everyone found their own best vantage point to see a painting and respectfully maneuvered themselves around other visitors. Visitors spoke in hushed tones.

You feel transported at both places. The Butterfly Conservatory was a calm and relaxing place. You feel transported from any worries you might have. Similarly at the art exhibition I found myself transported by paintings. I asked myself, How does the artist's painting make me feel? What inspired the artist to paint their painting?

The Butterfly Conservatory in Niagara Falls is a hidden gem. It opened in 1996 and yet I just learned about this place a couple of weeks ago.

If you are planning a trip to Niagara Falls, be sure to visit the Butterfly Conservatory. It's a short 20–25 minute bus ride from Clifton Hill (a famous attraction in Niagara Falls) to the Butterfly Conservatory. Once there, you can see colourful and beautiful butterflies in a natural lush setting. You feel transported. Any worries you might have disappear in this place that inspires awe and curiosity.

Serendipitous Moment

I remember the first day on the job at the Y.

It wasn't that long ago.

I was scheduled to start at 9:00 a.m.

I got there early.

The front door to the Y wouldn't even be open yet.

The Y is located in an office building in mid-town Toronto.

After pacing the hall, I decided to look at the building directory.

I was curious to see who the other tenants were.

One of the names was a dentist.

This person had the same name as a girl I knew in high school. At the time she said that she wanted to become a dentist. What were the chances that the dentist's name on the building directory would be the same person I knew from high school?

On my second day on the job, I decided to venture out on my lunch break and see if the dentist on the 6th floor was the same person I knew from high school.

When I stepped into the office, I spoke to the receptionist, who said that the dentist wasn't in yet. Come back in 10 minutes.

Undeterred, I went downstairs and came back up again in 10 minutes.

When the dentist arrived at the office, I didn't recognize her at first, but as we started talking I could tell that it was the same person I went to high school with.

She didn't recognize me either.

I started to name some of the people we played euchre with at lunchtime and I noted a glimmer of recognition.

The big news that she shared was that she is retiring from dentistry at the end of the year.

Here I was, starting a new job, and she was retiring from hers.

It's a small world that a high school classmate of mine would have an office in the same building where I work.

I marvel about the what-ifs: What if I hadn't looked at the building directory? Or, what if I hadn't returned to the 6th floor for the second time?

If I weren't so curious or persistent, I would not have reconnected with my classmate.

We create our own serendipitous moments sometimes.

Universal Truth

I shared with a friend that I like to do yoga and run life-affirming quotes in my head in the morning.

I felt compelled to mention at least one quote that I consider life-affirming and by chance I mentioned a Winnie-the-Pooh quote:

"You are braver than you believe, you are stronger than you seem and you are smarter than you think." —A.A. Milne

My friend wrote back and shared a short story that he wrote using Winnie-the-Pooh characters.

Who knew that my friend thought about Winnie-the-Pooh too?

I liked his story. He's a very creative guy.

I've been noticing a particular commercial on television.

In this commercial, they partially quote Winnie-the-Pooh:

"You are braver than you believe, you are stronger than you seem…"

For the life of me, I don't remember who is sponsoring the commercial or what the commercial is about, but I was excited to hear a Winnie-the-Pooh quote in a commercial!

I talked about this commercial with my friend.

He hadn't seen the commercial, but he's heard the commercial somewhere.

It's funny what you remember sometimes.

Yesterday I did some overtime at work.

It was a quarter to five and I thought about getting something to eat.

I know of a little tuck shop down the hallway.

On my way there I glanced over to see what was playing at the movie theatre.

"Goodbye Christopher Robin."

Christopher Robin is a character in Winnie-the-Pooh.

I didn't know that this movie existed nor that it was playing at this movie theatre.

It's funny how something can enter your consciousness and you start noticing it everywhere.

I told a friend something about myself: I like Winnie-the-Pooh quotes. I was delighted that Winnie-the-Pooh happened to resonate with this friend.

You could say that Winnie-the-Pooh has made our connection stronger.

When you throw something positive out in the universe, you just might receive something positive and amazing in return. You just never know.

Playing Nice in the Sandbox

As a new employee there is so much to think about.

One of the things that I'm thinking about is making sure that I get along with my colleagues.

This week I was debriefed on the Myers-Briggs personality test that I took a couple of months ago before being hired.

I found out that I'm an introvert.

I suspected as much.

This particular personality test says that there are 16 personality types.

With all these different personality types, how do people manage to get along?

I attended a workshop this week where the facilitator talked about "checking your ego at the door."

I think that's one way for people to get along at work.

"Check your ego at the door."

It's not always about me.

What I may perceive as a slight from a co-worker may not have been intended as a slight at all.

It's just their work style or a miscommunication.

They could be having a bad day.

Or I could be having a bad day.

I remind myself to give people the benefit of the doubt and to not take things personally.

Also helpful: know thyself, keep calm, respect others, keep an open mind, understand where people are coming from, find common ground, have empathy for others.

Another way for people to get along at work is to take the company's values to heart and to treat each other in the same spirit as espoused by company values.

Our company's values include caring, health, honesty, inclusiveness, respect and responsibility.

I definitely believe and live by these values. I see these values demonstrated by my colleagues every day.

I learned at my debriefing that too much of something could be a bad thing.

You need a balance.

While it's good to be reflective, you need to let loose sometimes.

I appreciate my colleagues.

Let's have a good time and share a laugh.

Know Thyself

Before being hired at my current company I was asked to take the VIA Survey (personality assessment).

This assessment says that everyone has 24 character strengths, but that a couple of character strengths will show up as being dominant for an individual.

My top two character strengths are kindness and honesty.

To be honest, if you are looking for a job (or you just want to increase your self-awareness), you might want to look into taking the VIA Survey.

It's free to take the survey, but there's a cost if you would like to receive a report that describes your particular character strengths.

You can take the survey at viacharacter.org.

It's helpful to know who you are and what's important to you, because you can decide if your values coincide with the values of the company you are applying to.

My company's values include caring, health, honesty, inclusiveness, respect and responsibility.

I'm lucky that my strongest character strengths (kindness and honesty) coincide with my company's values (caring and honesty).

I think I'm going to like where I work.

Receiving confirmation of what your dominant character strengths are can help you to work on increasing those character strengths.

I try to be kind and serve other people.

Just the other day at work, I noticed that someone spilled liquid on the lunchroom floor. Being the health and safety person that I am, I just wiped it up... I didn't want anyone to slip on the spilled liquid.

You also need to be kind to yourself.

Sometimes I have the tendency to beat myself up (mentally). I stop, notice what I'm doing and tell myself to stop that! ☺

Give and take is important. You can burn yourself out if you are constantly being kind and giving in a relationship. Think about how the other person in a relationship is giving and if you need to balance things out. If you need to re-balance a relationship, you can approach that in a kind way.

I've always prided myself on being honest.

For example, being transparent is important to me. In one of my posts "S is for Stress", I write about how starting a new job was stressing me out.

I try not to be blunt. I tend to think before I talk. I'm a diplomatic kind of guy.

I think it was a gift that I was asked to take the VIA Survey.

It reminded me of who I think I am.

It made me pause and think of what small actions I can take to be more of who I think I am.

I would like to think that I am kind and honest.

Spirit of Christmas

Every year I go to my local Hallmark store and shop for boxed Christmas cards.

I choose Christmas cards that seem to "pop" out at me and hope that the Christmas card that I send "pops" out to the recipient as well.

When I was at Combined Insurance, I worked on four different Committees.

I'd give a Christmas card to everyone I worked with on those Committees, plus all my colleagues in the HR department (that was about 25–30 Christmas cards in total).

Recently at work I gave a Christmas card to each of my HR colleagues and I mailed a few Christmas cards to friends. I gave 25–30 Christmas cards this year.

In my heart I send Christmas cards as a way to say "hi, how are you?"; "thank you" and "I appreciate you"!

It makes me happy to send out Christmas cards.

Christmas has a personal meaning to each of us, but it can be a time for spending time with family and friends and being kind to one another.

The spirit of Christmas (kindness) is something that we can keep with us and demonstrate every day of the year.

We can think about the following:

What is one kind thing that we can do for someone today?

What is one kind thing that we can do for ourselves today?

If you're like me, I keep a gratitude journal and I think:

What is one kind thing that happened to me today?

We can be kind to one another and to ourselves.

I wish you a Merry Christmas and Happy New Year!

Keep well!

And see you in 2018!

Play It, Sam!

Your friends help to broaden your horizons.

I meet with my friend every couple of months to play backgammon or cribbage.

My friend taught me how to play backgammon.

I taught my friend how to play cribbage.

The other day I met up with my friend.

We went to a restaurant that he introduced me to.

We go there quite often.

These meet-ups are a chance to catch up with what's going on with the other.

I opened the conversation.

I couldn't wait to tell my friend.

Near the end of the evening, he announced that he was taking piano lessons.

For a month.

With news like that, I wouldn't have been able to contain myself.

When I was a child I studied piano.

For 10 years.

I got as far as Grade 8.

That's pretty good, considering the highest grade is Grade 10.

I liked the freedom of playing the piano.

When I played, it was like entering a state of flow.

You focus on what you're doing and forget about everything else.

I played in recitals.

These were terrifying events.

I was afraid of hitting the wrong key or forgetting my music.

I did both.

And you live to tell the story.

All of a sudden I stopped playing the piano.

I was 18.

I wasn't enjoying it anymore.

I reached a plateau.

I wasn't going to become a professional piano player or teacher.

It was time to pursue other interests.

My friend was excited that he mastered a piece.

So much so he posted his debut performance on social media.

I was excited for my friend.

And proud that he is trying something new.

Sometimes his interests become my interests.

And my interests become his interests.

Maybe it's time to open up the sheet music again.

So, "Play it, Sam!"

This is a quote from "Casablanca."

And I couldn't wait to tell you.

Smile

I wrote a post called "Mentors" about how mentors are all around us if only we were to take notice.

Your colleagues can be your best mentors. Or, you can act as your own best mentor.

A friend of mine, Marc Belaiche, commented on the post:

"It's funny... sometimes mentors don't even know how they helped change someone's life!"

Marc's comment made me smile, because I hadn't thought of his perspective when I was writing the post.

He's right that someone may regard you as their mentor and you don't even know it.

Marc's comment reminded me of a small moment that I experienced recently.

I take the subway to work every morning and get off at the Eglinton subway station.

Every morning commuters are greeted by the sounds of subway musicians at this station.

Usually I don't take notice of the subway musicians, but on January 22nd, my ears perked up.

Two older musicians were playing the song "Smile" (music by Charlie Chaplin and lyrics by John Turner and Geoffrey Parsons).

One was playing the saxophone; the other was playing the accordion.

They were a killer combination.

> "Smile though your heart is aching
>
> Smile even though it's breaking
>
> When there are clouds in the sky, you'll get by
>
> If you smile through your fear and sorrow
>
> Smile and maybe tomorrow
>
> You'll see the sun come shining through for you"

After I left the station I was humming the song and still humming the song when I arrived at the office.

They made my day.

When I got home, I regretted that I didn't give a tip to these musicians.

I wondered if I would ever see these musicians again.

A week later at the same place and time, I saw the same two subway musicians.

They were playing a different song that I wasn't familiar with.

This time I showed my appreciation and gave them five dollars.

They made my day on January 22nd.

They made me smile.

And they didn't even know it.

Put a Song in Your Heart

I collect programs of all the musicals that I've seen over the years. There have been many. I share some of my favourite musicals in this post.

Most recently I saw *Come From Away* at the Royal Alexandra Theatre (Feb 17th). I was moved by the humanity that shines through in this story about the folks of Gander, Newfoundland, who took in 7000 stranded air travellers on 9/11. This musical moves at break-neck speed. You learn a lot about the characters in just 100 minutes through songs and stories. This musical made me proud to be a Canadian. This musical is playing in Toronto until September 2018. I recommend it!

I wanted to see *Beautiful—The Carole King Musical* because I really like "You've Got a Friend." I got to hear this song near the end of the musical. I was introduced to some songs that I didn't know Carole King wrote. I enjoyed all the songs in this musical.

Another one of my favourite songs is "Can't Take My Eyes Off You," which they sing in *Jersey Boys*. You could say that I'm a Frankie Valli fan. I liked this musical, saw the movie and saw Frankie Valli a couple of times live in concert. This musical played at the Toronto Centre for the Arts in North York. When I bought the tickets, I didn't know where we'd be sitting. When I arrived at the theatre, I was disappointed that the seats were in the front row! I'd have to be looking up throughout the entire performance. I went to the box office and asked if I could exchange my tickets and they obliged! We ended up sitting in the rear orchestra which were better seats!

I saw *Mamma Mia* not once but twice at the Royal Alexandra Theatre! I guess you could say that I can't get enough of ABBA. One of my favourite ABBA songs is "Take a Chance On Me."

Les Misérables is such a dramatic and sweeping musical. I like "I Dreamed a Dream" and "Master of the House," which is a lesser-known song from this musical.

The first (of two) musicals that I saw on Broadway was *Dreamgirls*. It was a thrill to see a Broadway musical!

One of the greatest musicals of all time is *The King and I*. I'm a little biased as I was in this production as one of the Royal Children.

Being in *The King and I* was a memorable experience that got me interested in this art form at a young age.

Cheers to the musical that brings people together to share a once-in-a-lifetime experience!

Confessions of a Newbie Worker

This new job is a challenge.

Two weeks ago I implemented a tickler file system at work to help keep me organized.

I'm feeling more organized now.

Now I'm feeling that there is so much to do and not enough time to do it in.

Every day last week I worked 1.5–2.0 hours past my official finish time.

I used to do this when I was at Combined Insurance (2005–2013), but at that time I felt there was an expectation to work overtime.

This time around there isn't an expectation to work overtime, but if I don't I'll fall behind.

I can take comfort that I tackled the most important things that needed to get done.

I am getting sh*t done, for sure!

At the end of each day last week I was mentally exhausted.

I was getting into a habit of going to the deli down the hall at 3:45 p.m. and buying a sugary snack (banana cake, muffin, date square).

I can feel my heart rate surge, or maybe that's stress.

I am aware that I need to avoid the sugary snack ritual and I'm making some inroads in that regard.

I'm reminded of a quote by Robin Sharma:

"All change is hard at first, messy in the middle and so gorgeous at the end."

I feel like I'm in the middle of that trajectory.

When I was at Combined Insurance, all I thought about was work.

I don't want to make that same mistake twice.

I am seeking a balance.

In the morning I meditate and do some yoga for 5–7 minutes.

I'll go for a walk when the weather gets nicer.

It also helps to talk about your feelings.

A Little Good News—Part I

On March 17th I presented myself to the local Emergency department.

I'd been experiencing a rapid heartbeat for the past couple of days and chalked it up to eating too much sugar.

Finally I took some advice from my loved ones and went to the hospital.

The nurse asked me questions.

In addition to rapid heartbeat, I was experiencing fatigue and chills.

I was quickly diagnosed as having hyperthyroidism.

I was admitted to the hospital and stayed for a day.

Upon discharge I was given an appointment to see a specialist (endocrinologist).

The appointment with the specialist is tomorrow.

It's been an interesting challenge between March 17th and April 10th.

In this period I developed shortness of breath.

It's a terrifying sensation to feel that you can't breathe.

I presented myself to Emergency four times.

The doctors tried Ventolin therapy.

Unfortunately my body didn't respond to this therapy.

I tried to relax.

I concentrated on my breathing.

I breathed in through my nose for 2 seconds and exhaled through my mouth for 3 seconds.

I repeated the cycle.

I sat in a chair and leaned over with my elbows to my knees.

These techniques helped me to relax.

I told friends and colleagues of my health challenge.

Maybe they knew of people who had thyroid issues?

Did those people have good outcomes?

I was open to hearing advice.

"Drink lots of water."

"Get plenty of rest."

I appreciated the advice.

In advance of tomorrow's appointment, I did some research on thyroid issues and thought of some questions to ask.

I came across the Thyroid Foundation of Canada web site.

I found the information presented there to be helpful.

At tomorrow's appointment I'm hoping to hear how I can manage this issue.

I'm open to hearing any news.

Any news would be good news to help me move forward.

A Little Good News—Part 2

I wrote a LinkedIn post called **A Little Good News** and talked about my health challenge with hyperthyroidism.

At the end of the post I talked about having an initial appointment with an endocrinologist on April 11th.

Prior to the appointment I felt a bit of fear of the unknown.

I could be diagnosed with thyroiditis or Graves' disease.

I knew with Graves' disease that I could be put on antithyroid medication.

Thyroiditis seemed to be a little less severe.

At my appointment I was diagnosed with thyroiditis (inflammation of the thyroid gland and a type of hyperthyroidism).

I was informed that with thyroiditis that my thyroid level will return to normal on its own.

I don't need to be put on any antithyroid medication.

This was good news.

The endocrinologist mentioned that my hyperthyroidism might have been triggered by a viral infection that I had last year.

I thought to myself that the viral infection might have been caused by a low immune system, and that my low immune system might have come about (partly) because of the stress that I was perceiving in my job.

Everything connects to one another.

To help myself I've begun to think about how I can reduce my stress so that I don't become sick again.

I've begun meditation.

I came across a University Health Network video on the Workplace Strategies for Mental Health web site.

It talks about a breathing exercise you can do.

It's very simple.

Breathe in slowly through your nose for 2 seconds. Hold your breath briefly. Exhale slowly through your mouth for 3 seconds. Pause. Repeat the cycle. Be conscious of your breathing. You can close your eyes if you want.

I de-cluttered this weekend.

I organized my work space at home and threw away things that I no longer need.

I already feel a calming effect.

I am going to change my early morning routine so that I get to work 10 minutes earlier.

Maybe this 10 minutes will help so that I don't have to stay as late after work.

I am on the lookout for articles on stress management.

I came across an article on the Canadian Mental Health Association web site called "10 Tips on How to De-stress at Work."

I love reading Eric Barker's blog "Barking Up the Wrong Tree."

I'll check out his blog for stress management articles.

I am scheduled for blood tests within the next three months.

At the end of three months I will visit the endocrinologist for a recheck.

I hope that the things that I am doing to reduce my stress will translate into a normal thyroid level.

One can only hope.

Window of Opportunity

I lost my job last week.

But I learned a few things from this experience.

I learned to organize myself better.

I divided my day into chunks of time and focused my attention on one task in the morning and another task in the afternoon.

There really wasn't enough time in the day.

I challenged myself and made it a game to get into work a half-hour earlier (@ 8:00 a.m.) and have more time to get a few more things done.

I became more self-aware about self-care.

I took a moment to do a few deep breathing exercises throughout the day and alleviated stress in the process.

I became comfortable with working with Excel pivot tables.

Prior to this job I trembled at the thought of doing pivot tables, but I received some training and it was a matter of diving in and trying it out.

You can teach an old dog new tricks.

I came into the job really open to learning and learning how things were done.

I felt vulnerable at the start because I wasn't versed on department policies and procedures.

I had helpful colleagues who showed me the way.

I've been reading up on Buddhist philosophy.

Nothing in life stays the same.

We can become empowered to help ourselves.

We can reframe a situation, take one small step forward towards our goal, and keep persistent and not give up.

I contacted a former employer and asked to be kept in mind for any future opportunities.

As chance would have it, there was a current opening for which I received an interview.

I'll receive some news soon.

"Focus on what matters (most). Where attention goes, energy flows. Where energy flows, things grow." —Marc & Angel Chernoff, Professional Coaches

I'll focus on opening another door.

And creating a window of opportunity.

Circles

I admire my friends who speak two or more languages.

They act like a bridge between cultures.

A close friend of mine from Iran lives in Toronto.

Whenever I have a question about Iran, I ask my friend. Through the years I've learned something about Iranian culture from my friend. He is an Iranian ambassador in those moments.

Similarly people he knows from Iran may have questions about Canada. In answering these questions, he is a Canadian ambassador in those moments.

Like I said, a bridge between cultures.

I don't speak another language (other than English), but I think I am a bridge when it comes to age.

My friends range in age from their 20s to 80s.

Sometimes I think I have a Millennial outlook.

I'm interested in AI and how that might impact work. Doing meaningful work is important to me. Being open and transparent are important to me.

I can relate to my own Boomer generation.

I know who Lawrence Welk is. And a rotary telephone.

I bring my Millennial sensibilities when I'm in conversation with Boomers or Traditionalists. Similarly I bring my Boomer sensibilities when I'm in conversation with Millennials.

You and I run in different social circles.

When I join up with you in conversation I'm bringing influences from my different social circles and facets of myself into the conversation.

A conversation is an opportunity for us to learn something about each other and find something in common.

We are all interconnected.

This is a Buddhist philosophy thing.

As well as six degrees of separation.

The title of this post reminds me of a Captain and Tennille song.

Who is Captain and Tennille, you ask?

That's a Boomer thing. ☺

Back to the Future

I'm thinking about what to do next in my career.

Employment consulting (i.e., helping people in their job searches) seems like a good fit to me.

I think back to a summer job that I had at Senior Link and wonder what it was about that job that I liked so much.

I was 18 at the time.

I was going to seniors' homes and performing chores like cutting the grass, mopping the floor, painting a fence.

I learned about **building relationships** in this summer job by being a friendly ear and just listening. I took pride in the fact that I gained regular customers who would ask for me by name to come over and do some chores.

I like **helping people,** and I helped seniors to live independently in their own homes.

This job did not feel like a job to me.

I got to be who I am. This job required patience and I was (and still am) a patient person. I worked with three other students who were doing a similar job. I felt there was a lot of camaraderie on our team. On occasion I'd double up with a colleague on a job that was too much for one person. Those occasions were fun.

More recently I enjoy helping friends who are in a job search. This could mean forwarding an article that may be of interest to them, introducing one friend to another friend on LinkedIn or just spending some time and doing a coffee meet-up.

In 2017 I worked at the Ontario Society of Senior Citizens Organizations. I had the opportunity of presenting 4 job search workshops and helping older unemployed workers (50–70). I have a lot of empathy for "older" workers as I am an older worker myself. I've had 24+ years experience in Human Resources and I was very excited to share my knowledge as to how a recruiter thinks.

I find myself drawn to anything related to employment and how job seekers may wish to take care of themselves. I read books, articles and listen to podcasts on self care, precarious employment, future of work, AI, workforce innovation, etc.

I feel I would be suited to employment consulting because of who I am (care about people and working on their behalf), my skills (relationship management, communication and facilitation skills) and continuous desire to learn all things related to employment.

The video link that I attached to this post is Huey Lewis & the News' "Power of Love (Theme from Back to the Future)", which is appropriate because sometimes you need to look back in order to move forward.

www.ingramcontent.com/pod-product-compliance
Lightning Source LLC
Chambersburg PA
CBHW020424220526
45464CB00002B/551